MANAGEMENT

Alberto Silva

MANAGEMENT

ISBN 978-0-9915219-4-4

ISBN 978-0-9915219-3-7 (ebook)

Cognitio
Books & Apps

www.cognitiobooks.com

Table of Contents

INTRODUCTION

THE CONCEPT OF MANAGEMENT

Management is defined as the utilization of available resources by a manager with the goal of achieving the objectives or goals of an organization.

Management encompasses the administration of all types of organizations: armies, businesses, governments, hospitals, hotels, nonprofit organizations, schools, sport teams, etc. Although management is so varied, there are several fundamental principles which are presented in this book.

Management is studied in universities at different levels, but mainly in master's programs in business administration (MBA) or management. The fundamental management courses in many university business programs, some mandatory and some elective, are the same as the topics covered in this book: organizational behavior, human resource management, organizational change, leadership development, managerial communication, project management, strategic planning and implementation, and developing a business plan. In addition to these fundamental management courses, programs often include classes on finance, international business, marketing, operations, and technology, depending on the nature of the programs and student interest.

PURPOSE OF THE BOOK

The intent of this book is to provide a quick and easy guide for students in MBA or similar programs to navigate within these subjects with regard to their specific area of management. It can also serve as companion to the textbooks used in those programs.

Besides serving as a support for graduate studies, this book can also be useful as a reference manual for practicing managers who wish to gain an overview of the concepts and theories related to their activities.

Although some duplication of topics between courses often exists, this has been avoided or reduced in this text. For example, aspects of change and leadership that are common components of organizational behavior courses are treated separately.

To facilitate the reading and understanding of this book, references are omitted; however, the author acknowledges his debt to all of the contributors and invites the reader to delve into each topic using the many fine sources available. A short bibliography is offered at the end of the book.

CHAPTER 1

ORGANIZATIONAL BEHAVIOR

ORGANIZATIONAL BEHAVIOR

Organizational behavior is a field of study in which the conduct of people in organizations is investigated.

As a field of study, organizational behavior has benefitted from the research and contributions of many sciences (psychology, sociology, anthropology, political science, etc.).

The purpose of the study of organizational behavior is to be able to achieve forms of behavior in an organization that promote the achievement of its objectives. Among the many issues addressed by the study of organizational behavior are the following:

- What influences individual behavior at work?
- What should be done to ensure that employees are motivated and perform at maximum capacity?
- What makes employees stressed and what can be done to prevent it?
- What should be done to encourage teamwork in the organization?
- How should conflict be handled?
- What should be done to improve communication between people?
- What is the most appropriate structure for a given organization?

- What should be done to help the organization make better decisions?

ORGANIZATIONAL CULTURE

Organizational culture is the set of shared beliefs and values by members of an organization.

Culture is the style of thinking, feeling, and reacting to problems that are shared by members of an organization and is transmitted to new members over time. Culture has a strong influence in the way people behave within an organization and changes gradually as a result of the actions of the members of that organization.

The culture of an organization is largely intangible, so it is not possible to know an organization's culture in depth without studying or living in it for a considerable time. It is easy to see very superficial aspects of culture, such as office design, the dress of the employees, established rules, and formal practices; but the deeper aspects such as values, norms, beliefs, and assumptions shared by members of the organization cannot be perceived as easily.

Some cultures are strong, characterized by many employees sharing their core values. However in weak cultures, few employees share the core values and different cultures within the organization begin to emerge. Although a very strong culture can be a barrier to change and innovation, in general it is preferable that organizational culture is strong and employees share common values.

Besides dividing organizational cultures into strong and weak, we can classify them in many different ways. For example, a generally accepted classification divides them into:

- Bureaucratic cultures (with an emphasis on rules, policies, procedures, chain of command, and centralized decision making).

- Cultures of clan (with an emphasis on affiliation, traditions, and rituals).

- Entrepreneurship cultures (with an emphasis on innovation, creativity, risk-taking, and aggressive pursuit of opportunities).

- Results oriented cultures (with an emphasis on increasing sales, increasing market share, financial stability, and profitability).

None of these types of culture is superior to the others. The most appropriate culture depends on the nature and purpose of an organization and the environment in which it operates. Moreover, although one of the above usually dominates, in most business organizations we usually find a mixture of these four types.

Sometimes, a change of organizational culture may be needed. For example, a company with bureaucratic or results oriented culture may consider it desirable to become a company with an entrepreneurial culture.

Cultural change is no easy task and requires much time, effort, and commitment from its top executives and the entire organization. It is necessary to establish the kind of culture that is required, convince all members of the organization of the need and desire for change, and move forward with insistence and perseverance in the desired direction. The leaders of an organization must ensure that the change is consistent, that all components of the organization are properly adjusted, and that people who strive to behave as expected are given proper recognition. Sometimes it may be necessary to replace some individuals with people who are a better fit for the new culture.

INDIVIDUAL DIFFERENCES

The behavior of people within an organization depends on individual differences. People differ in many respects, but the variables with the greatest influence on their behavior at work are:

- Hereditary and diversity factors (differences in age, ethnicity, gender, physical attributes, race, sexual or affectional orientation).

- Capacities (a person's natural talent to perform mental or physical tasks) and abilities (learned talents that a person acquires to perform a task).

Hereditary factors, diversity factors, capacities, and abilities are combined with individual psychological variables (personality, values, perception, attribution, and emotion) to give rise to attitudes or dispositions towards certain types of behavior, which can also be considered as individual differences.

A. Personality

Personality is the set of characteristics and individual differences that distinguish one person from another. These characteristics, called personality traits, are relatively stable and make a person behave in a certain way in a given situation. Some personality traits are inherited, but some are acquired during life experience.

Different variables have been proposed to differentiate between the personalities of individuals, but one of the most accepted models is that of the "Big Five" dimensions, which is based on the following variables:

- Extraversion

- Agreeability

- Emotional stability (neuroticism)

- Motivation to achieve (conscientiousness)

- Openness to experience

In general, people who are outgoing, gentle, emotionally stable, motivated to achieve, and open to experience relate better with others and exhibit better performance at work.

In well-defined situations, most people tend to react the same way. However, when a situation is ambiguous and the people involved have differences in character, behavior differences are presented. Therefore, organization policies and systems are set to define situations that may arise, so as to minimize the impact of personality differences at work and ensure predictable behavior.

B. Attitude

Attitude is a person's disposition. Is his inclination to respond favorably or unfavorably to an object, event, person, or social group.

In general, attitude depends on our beliefs, feelings, and intentions. These factors influence our mood toward the work we do, the organization we belong to, and the people we work with.

Attitude influences behavior, but is not completely its determinant. For example, sometimes people agree to behave in a certain way although their attitude or mood is unfavorable toward this form of behavior. It also happens that some people are more consistent than others and their behavior is more consistent with their attitudes. Cognitive dissonance is any inconsistency between two or more attitudes or between attitudes and behavior.

C. Perception

Perception is the feeling that a person has about an event or situation. What one perceives can be radically different from objective reality. For example, no matter what managers or administrators think or say, what is most important is how employees see, perceive, and interpret these messages.

Our perceptions are greatly affected by our beliefs and feelings, but can be particularly influenced by the processes of attribution and emotion.

D. Attribution

Attribution is the allocation of responsibility for an event or situation to someone or something. Individuals can interpret if events occurring around them are caused by themselves or by an external cause. Sometimes people are wrong and, for example, erroneously attribute the cause of an event or situation to another person or some external factor, when the reality is that they themselves are responsible for what happens. Attribution errors often occur because people don't possess or seek sufficient information about a person or situation and therefore make judgments without firm foundations.

E. Emotion

Emotion is a conscious mental reaction of intense character. Some of the feelings commonly regarded as emotions are love, fear, hate, terror, grief, and joy. People differ greatly in terms of managing their emotions and some psychologists use the term "emotional intelligence" to describe the ability to manage one's own emotions, as well as those of others. Proper management of emotions requires learning to calm anxiety, control impulsivity, react appropriately to anger, improve our ability to relate to others, and respond appropriately to emotions, including unexpressed feelings.

MOTIVATION

Motivation is a person's drive to behave in a certain way. This drive usually determines the effort a person is willing to give to achieve a certain goal.

The motivation for work, in particular, plays an important role in the behavior of people in an organization. Motivated people, unlike those who are unmotivated, generally have positive behaviors characterized by high levels of dedication and commitment to the objectives of the organization.

A. Theories of motivation

Various theories or models have been proposed to try to explain what motivation is based on and how it occurs.

Need theories assume that people are motivated by their needs and try to determine the most important needs of individuals. The main need theories that have been proposed are the following:

- *Maslow's Hierarchy of Needs theory.* According to this theory, needs are part of a hierarchy. Lower level needs are physiological, whereas needs for self-fulfillment are of a higher level. People try to meet their most basic needs before directing behavior toward satisfying higher level needs.

- *Alderfer's ERC theory.* This researcher agrees with Maslow in that individual needs obey a hierarchy. However, the hierarchy of needs only comprises three sets of needs: existence (E), relations (R), and growth (G).

- *Herzberg's Two-Factor theory.* For this author, motivation depends on two factors: dissatisfaction factors needed to maintain a minimum level of "no dissatisfaction" (salary, job security, working conditions, social status, etc.), and satisfaction or motivational factors (achievement, recognition, responsibility, etc.).

- *McClelland's Theory of Learned Needs.* This theory suggests that many needs are learned, such as the needs for achievement, affiliation, and power.

Other motivation theories that have been proposed are:

- Vroom's Theory of Expectations. Vroom assumes that employees are more likely to be motivated when they perceive that their efforts will produce desired results.

- Adams' Equity theory. This theory supposes that individuals are motivated by the desire to be treated equitably.

- Locke's Goal-Setting theory. Locke claims that the behavior of an individual is determined by the goals he sets for himself.

While not a theory of motivation, strictly speaking, Skinner's Reinforcement theory proposes that behavior is caused by the environment. What controls the behavior of people are reinforcements (rewards and punishments). According to this theory, any positive consequence immediately following an action increases the possibility of recurrence.

Motivation is a very complex phenomenon, dependent on the characteristics of each individual and their circumstances. Therefore, the various theories that have been proposed only provide partial explanations of motivation and are valid only in certain circumstances.

B. Motivation for work

Although there are vast differences among the motivation of individuals, overall work motivation depends on employees':

- Perception that their personal needs are being satisfied (subsistence, security, affection, recognition, and self-fulfillment).

- Pleasure and contentment in the specific job that he does.

- Level of comfort with the company.

Many companies mistakenly base their motivation plans exclusively on employee compensation. Although good remuneration is essential to meet the basic needs of the individual, money is not the most important factor for motivation. People work for money. But more importantly, they work to have something meaningful in their lives. If compensation is good, but people do not have confidence in the organization and do not see deeper meaning in the work that they do, they may stay with the company until they get a better job, but they will hardly develop the loyalty or commitment that would enable them to perform exceptionally.

STRESS AT WORK

Stress is the physical or mental impairment that an individual suffers as a result of subjecting his or herself to overwork, emotional strain, etc.

The degree of stress that an event produces does not only depend on the event itself, it also depends on the individual interpretation of the event. Consequently, people react differently to events or stressors and suffer different effects as a result of these events.

In general, people with strong personalities and who are relatively insensitive (type A) feel less stress and generally survive the pressures of organizational life more successfully, but usually at the cost of damaging interpersonal relationships that would make the organization more effective and more tolerable. They can even kill themselves in the process. Extreme type A behavior is associated with several important risk factors for health.

Stress manifests itself in several ways, usually in the form of physiological, psychological, or behavioral changes. Moderate stress stimulates the body and increases the ability to react. Indeed, positive stress, which is derived from a pleasurable event, is related to job satisfaction. Too much stress or unattainable demands, on the other hand, impose restrictions on individuals and their performance will suffer as a result.

In addition to decreasing productivity, people can become ill as a result of stress. Stress can cause back pain, headaches, stomach and intestinal problems, respiratory infections, mental problems, coronary heart disease, and possibly cancer.

Stressors are actions, situations, or events that place special demands on a person. The major stressors at work are:

- Role conflict
- Overwork
- Change
- Intragroup and intergroup relations

- Policies and organizational culture

- Downsizing

Stress accumulates. Thus, a stressor may be unimportant in itself, but if very high levels of stress are added, it can become "the straw that breaks the camel's back".

The best way to deal with stress is to deal with the cause. Events are generally less stressful when people think they can predict or control them.

People with greater emotional stability, confidence, and social support have better possibilities of coping well with stress. Some strategies to help deal with stressors include:

- Taking days off

- Learning relaxation techniques

- Finding support in friends and family

- Avoiding difficult people

- Practicing regular exercise

- Reading books that are not work-related

- Learning to manage time well

- Training to improve competencies

DECISION MAKING

Decisions are choices that are made between two or more alternatives to achieve something or solve a problem.

Managers are constantly required to make decisions in organizations: defining objectives, goals, and strategies; initiating and leading new projects to improve organizational performance; handling crisis situations and emergencies; hiring, promoting, compensating, and firing people; allocating human, material, and financial resources to different activities; negotiating with customers and other business units; etc.

Depending on these decisions, the objectives of an organization can be achieved and the behavior of people within an organization can become positive. If people do not have confidence in a manager's ability to make decisions and they feel that they are not allowed to participate in the decision making process, the organizational climate will be negatively affected.

A. Classification of decisions

We can use different criteria to classify decisions. One of these criteria divides them into following two types:

- *Programmed decisions.* Repetitive and routine decisions, with a clear, established procedure to resolve or address them

- *Unprogrammed decisions.* Innovative decisions, without a clear procedure for resolving or addressing them

Of course, the toughest decisions are those that have not been programmed, such as those involving many crisis situations and emergencies or those dealing with difficult ethical dilemmas. But some programmed decisions can also be difficult and critical, such as selecting an employee from a list of eligible candidates or promoting someone among several possible options to a key position.

B. Decision making processes

Sometimes decisions can be made following a rational process of development, evaluation, and selection of alternatives, using quantitative methods to facilitate it. However, most business decisions are not made in a logical and rational way. Uncertainty, time pressure, incomplete information, limited human resources, prejudice, and many other factors can affect the decision-making process and lead to the decline of rationality and the use of intuition or hunches in this process, sometimes with the unavoidable risk of making bad decisions.

C. Group decisions

In general, decisions made by groups are better than those made by individuals. One advantage of group decision making is that it can facilitate both the identification of risks and the generation of creative and innovative solutions. Group decisions can also facilitate the implementation of decisions, since the people involved in the process will be more willing to cooperate in executing the decisions.

Employees' participation in decision making:

• Is generally more feasible in unprogrammed decisions than in programmed decisions.

• Requires that they possess the information needed to make decisions.

• Tends to improve employee engagement in decision making.

• May not be advisable if any risk of conflict in the decision making process is anticipated.

In group decision making, it is important to note that discrepancy should be allowed and even encouraged. It is essential that the decision-making group encourages disagreement and confrontation of ideas and opinions in order to avoid the risks of groupthink (the illusion of invulnerability, the illusion of morality, pressure to conform, etc.).

It is also important to remember that group decision making does not mean that whoever leads or represents the group is exempt from responsibility in the decision. He is ultimately responsible. The intention to discuss the problem with his colleagues or others simply indicates the desire to gather more alternatives by adding the experiences and insight of different people.

TEAMWORK

In modern organizations, no important objective can be achieved individually. Hence the need for groups working to achieve different objectives: solve problems, implement projects, create new products, improve processes, etc. However, the mistake of confusing a working group with a team is often made. For a working group to become a team, its members need to cooperate closely and complement each other to achieve a common goal.

The effectiveness of a team depends on many factors including:

- The selection of the members, so that despite the convenience of a small team size, there is an adequate diversity of talents, skills, values, and personalities in accordance with the purpose intended.

- The appointment of a competent leader who is proven and able to gain the trust and respect of team members and of the rest of the organization.

- The definition of a common purpose, with clear, achievable, and shared objectives as well as the definition of collective and individual responsibility for achieving these objectives.

- The organizational support of the team, particularly from senior management, regarding allocation of resources, provision of information, and collaboration from other units when this is required by the team.

- The availability of time for learning processes and team building.

- An environment of trust and commitment within the team, with freedom and autonomy for its members in the execution of their tasks.

- Frequent communication and exchange of information among team members.

- The integration of the complementary skills of the team members to achieve their objectives.

The leader's ability to manage conflicts that may arise during the team's performance.

It is important to note that compensation systems and performance evaluations that emphasize individual goals or incentives, which unfortunately happens in many organizations, are a disadvantage to teamwork.

Virtual teams present special challenges, due to the relative isolation of their members. The leaders of these teams must make significant efforts, usually supported by good information systems and communication technology, to maintain motivation, cohesion, and team effectiveness.

CONFLICT MANAGEMENT

A conflict is a difficult situation that arises as a result of disagreement between people.

Discrepancy or disagreement between people is something inherent to human nature. Complex organizations with high member diversity are more likely to have innumerable conflicts within them. Therefore, people should learn to live with conflict and understand that it is natural and not necessarily bad.

Conflict, when not reaching excessive levels of confrontation, is a sign that the organization is alive and that people who work in it are free to express their ideas and feelings. The total absence of conflict may indicate a lack of energy and enthusiasm as well as a fear in people to say what they really think or feel.

Discrepancy, defined as the diversity of opinions and points of view, is necessary in organizations. The existence of too much agreement between senior managers may be the cause of failure for many organizations. The divergence of opinions, when discussed in an atmosphere of trust and respect, usually improves the quality of decisions, stimulates creativity and innovation, arouses interest and curiosity among the members of a group or organization, provides the means so that problems can be aired and tensions released, and creates an environment of self-evaluation and change.

However, there is also sufficient evidence that conflict often produces harmful results. For example, some people have a very low tolerance for disagreement. In that case, personal conflict impairs energy and demoralizes the spirit. Too many conflicts are detrimental, generate chaos, and harm personal relationships. Unproductive conflicts are called dysfunctional, as opposed to functional conflicts which, as we have seen, can be used to improve the performance of an organization.

When organizational conflict is excessive, the occurrence of communication problems, rivalries, recurrence at higher levels to resolve disputes, proliferation of rules and regulations, frustration, and inefficiency are frequently observed.

Since conflicts are usually inevitable in an organization, it is important to manage them well. Conflict management must begin by considering the nature and causes of the conflicts. There are many possible causes of organizational conflict, but the most likely are differences between people, differences in goals for different units and individuals, injustice and inequity, and lack of flexibility in dealing with personal problems of employees.

People try to resolve conflicts in various ways. Some use coercion, trying to get away with what they want; others evade conflict by pleasing the person with whom they have a conflict, trying not to disturb them; and many try a negotiation strategy, trying to quickly reach agreement or to collaborate with the other to solve a problem together. Choosing the most appropriate method depends on the problem's consistency, both in personal preferences as well as situational considerations. Overall, the end result should be the successful resolution of the dispute.

Although not necessarily the most appropriate conflict resolution method in all situations, negotiation is a method frequently used in organizations. Negotiation is a process in which two or more parties try to reach an acceptable agreement in a situation characterized by some discomfort.

In the field of business, negotiation needs are numerous, for example:

- Between a company and its customers or suppliers to agree on the price, quality, and delivery date of products or services.

- Between the company and regulatory government agencies to agree on pricing or other terms of marketing products and services.

- Between the company and the unions to reach agreements on working conditions and remuneration.

- Among managers to make decisions and reach agreements in working relationships.

- Between a manager and his subordinates to agree on the objectives and conditions of the execution of work.

The ideal outcome of negotiations is generally a scheme in which each party wins without the other having a corresponding loss.

Some people use negotiation tactics based on manipulation, cunning, dissimulation, deception, or intimidation. However, centuries of diplomatic experience advise a more respectful behavior. A good negotiator:

- Never bases the success of his negotiations on false promises or breach of his word.

- Negotiates on a firm basis and pays utmost attention to the precise and complete wording of any agreement, leaving no room for doubt or interpretation difficulties of any kind.

- Remains calm throughout the negotiation process.

- Shows good character or is at least able to keep his temper under perfect control.

- Supports adversity and is always waiting for the right moment.

- Makes no presumption of merit and is able to shed his own opinion in order to put himself in the position of the person with whom he is negotiating.

- Is faithful to the organization or the interests that he represents, but is also loyal to his counterpart.

POWER AND POLITICS

Many people believe that politics is something that only has to do with government and elections to public office. The reality is that politics, the struggle for power, is present in human organizations of all kinds. Organizations are communities of people and therefore behave like other communities. In them, there is competition for power and resources, differences of opinion, conflicts of values, and priorities and goals.

To understand the nature of political activity in organizations, it is necessary to first distinguish between authority and power. Authority is the formal and official right of a manager to decide and act in the organization, according to his position. Power is the ability to influence others. This ability may or may not be consistent with authority. It can, and does occur with some frequency, that a person has more influence or power than what supposedly corresponds to his position in the organization. The contrary may also occur: a person, despite occupying an important position in the organization, has little power or influence due to his lack of interest or personal capacity.

In general, according to the position that a person occupies in the organization, he has a formal power (coercive power, reward power, legitimate power, information power, etc.), but regardless of that position, he may have a power based on unique individual characteristics (expert power, referent power or identification with the person, charismatic power).

Some of the main results from power studies include the following conclusions:

- The most common sources of power are authority and the control of resources.

- People with greater ability to acquire power have greater ease of expression, sensitivity, social skills, competence, and popularity.

- Power is generally achieved through conversation.

- Power is used more in conditions of scarcity of resources and for important resources or crucial decisions.

Empowerment is a process that has received much attention from researchers, finding that:

- There is a trend towards empowerment.

- There are different degrees of empowerment.

- Empowerment is usually due to the need to provide a fast, economical, and efficient service.

- Empowerment is generally beneficial to employee motivation.

- Empowerment requires information to act and demand accountability mechanisms

- In an organization, as is the case in the government of a country, those who have no power or want more power have to form coalitions. They associate with or bind to other people, sometimes even outside the organization, to try to occupy the highest executive positions and/or have more influence in the direction of the organization.

As a result of intense political activity and the changes that have occurred in organizations, management language itself has changed. For instance, instead of bosses, command, order, direct, and hierarchy, it is preferred to speak of leaders, convince, persuade, coordinate, and team.

While politics cannot be separated from the life of an organization, people can be uncomfortable and even threatened when they work in an environment with a high level of political behavior. This excess of political activity tends to occur more frequently in large, complex organizations and in advanced stages of the organizational life cycle or during resource shortages. In order to survive when political activity is excessive, some people choose to stay under the shadow of others who are perceived as stronger and they become their followers in order to feel safe; or they ignore the activities occurring around them and concentrate on their work. This environment, of course, can be harmful to the organization. To avoid excessive political activity, organizations should encourage open discussion of differences and constructive conflict management.

ORGANIZATIONAL STRUCTURE

Organizations should be designed. Although the organizational design is often confused with the definition of the structure, the latter activity is only part of organizational design. The design of an organization should be a proper arrangement of its various components: strategy, structure, people, management style, systems, and culture.

Organizational structure is the way to divide, organize, and coordinate the activities of an organization. It must be consistent with all other components of the organization so that it can efficiently achieve its goals.

A. Types of organizational structures

There are various forms of organizational structures from which companies can choose one that suits their nature and size. The main types of organizational structures are:

- *Simple structure.* This structure has only a manager and a core of workers that he personally directs. It is the typical structure of any small business run by its sole owner. Of course, the origin of this type of structure dates back many centuries. Despite the subsequent development of other more complex, and therefore more suitable structures for larger organizations, this structure remains probably the most used in the world as it is used frequently by thousands of micro and small enterprises everywhere.

- *Functional structure.* Activities are gathered around common functions from the base to the top of the organization. The most common functions in most organizations are marketing, finance, and operations/production. These functions are distinguished from support functions, such as planning and human resource management.

- *Division or multidivisional structure.* In this structure, the organization, usually a corporation, establishes divisions that are responsible for certain products, services, customer groups, or geographical areas.

- *Matrix structure.* This is a kind of structure that is team-based, with horizontal linkages between many employees working with a great deal of autonomy.

Apart from these traditional forms of organizational structures, new organizational structures or virtual structures exist. Although there is no single definition of virtual structure, it is generally accepted that this type of structure is characterized by:

- The existence of multiple bonds between individuals through networks within and outside the organization, facilitated by information technology and communication.

- Implementation of continuous processes of creation, dissemination and use of knowledge across the organization.

- The decline in importance of the departmental division and hierarchy.

- The structuring of work around workflows or processes.

- Work being carried out in teams, usually self-managed, which are continuously formed and dissolved.

- The operation of the organization as an open system, without clearly defined borders or boundaries, with resources that can be used anywhere, and frequent alliances or affiliate links with multiple individuals and external organizations.

- The concentration of the central organization in its core or distinctive competencies, using its extensive network of suppliers and partners to carry out the tasks that they can do better.

- The flexibility to modify the organizational structure in response to changes in environmental conditions.

The main differences between virtual and conventional structures have been identified as follows:

- Virtual structure is much flatter, with many traditional layers of middle management replaced by control areas that have a large span and are facilitated by technology.

- New organizational structures are focused on continuous learning, development of the core capabilities of the company, and flexibility

- New organizational structures are more decentralized, flexible, and innovation-oriented rather than efficiency-oriented

The emergence of virtual structures is attributed to the need for companies to improve their flexibility and adaptability in response to an increasingly chaotic environment.

Although many modern organizations have a conventional formal organizational structure coexisting with operating characteristics typical of virtual structures, there is no doubt that as the work in the organization becomes more virtual, the organizational form it takes differs more from conventional and should be considered a new organizational form.

B. Selection of the organizational structure

An organizational structure's level of convenience for a particular organization depends on the effectiveness of this type of structure for that organization. In any case, it is important to note that the structure should be subordinate to the work processes in the organization. For this reason, usually the first step in organizational design after the strategy is established is the design of work processes. This is followed by the definition of the structure, systems, and people to carry out these processes, as well as the management style most appropriate to the culture that is desired.

ETHICS IN ORGANIZATIONS

Ethics is defined as the distinction between good and bad: the belief that there are reasons to prefer one type of activity to another. People are free and can choose to have a virtuous life according to moral principles characterized by respect for humanity, or they can behave in any other way. But if one opts for a virtuous life, he must learn to distinguish good deeds from bad. To determine whether an action is good or bad, one must wonder what would happen if everyone behaved in that way. Therefore, murder, theft, rape, assault, torture, etc., are reprehensible actions. Such is the meaning of the famous categorical imperative proposed by the German philosopher Kant in the eighteenth century: "Act only according to that maxim whereby you can, at the same time, will that it should become a universal law."

Ethical behavior means that managers must comply with the laws and regulations that apply to the exercise of their activity, but it goes beyond the law. In particular, managers must base their action on the principles of justice and accountability. Justice implies a respect for all people inside and outside the organization, which is manifested in an honest and equitable relationship with all of them, seeking their welfare. Accountability is the responsibility for their actions and those of the people with whom they work, particularly if they are their subordinates.

The incorporation of ethics in decision making involves properly taking into account the possible consequences of a decision. The worst decisions are those that threaten the continuity of a company due to high financial losses, legal conflicts, and loss of legitimacy for breaches of social responsibility, as well as those that adversely affect the health or welfare of people. In such situations, managers must use their best professional judgment and ethical principles.

A company's code of ethics of may have some utility, but in general these codes have failed to prevent serious situations of corruption that have sometimes reached the scale of large public scandals. Increasingly, managers need to incorporate ethics in business decisions, but unfortunately, deception and greed often prevail.

CHAPTER 2

HUMAN RESOURCE MANAGEMENT

HUMAN RESOURCES

In order to exist and function, organizations need individuals who have been called at various times employees, personnel, staff, human resources, people, or human capital. Human resources, a term probably coined in the 1960s, remains the most frequently used to refer to the employees or individuals in an organization.

Organizations and the individuals who work in them have different needs; but for the organization to achieve its objectives, it must harmonize its needs with those of the employees. Some organizations achieve a good balance of their needs and those of their members, but in many others, balance is usually not achieved because of the indifference or incompetence of their managers.

Although all managers say their most important asset is their employees because they help to sustain the success of the companies they run, the reality is that there is a big gap between what is said and what is done in relation to the management of human resources. The truth is that the management of these human resources leaves much to be desired in most companies which privilege economic performance over the welfare of their people.

HUMAN RESOURCE MANAGEMENT

Human resource management (HRM) is the process of hiring, developing, motivating, and evaluating employees to achieve the goals of the company. This process includes the following activities:

- Planning

- Recruitment

- Selection

- Induction

- Training and development

- Performance evaluation

- Career planning

HUMAN RESOURCE PLANNING

Planning of human resources is the design of a strategy to achieve and maintain the human resources that are needed. The human resources plan must be based on the strategic plan and also must form an essential part of it.

In practice, given the uncertainty of today's world, many companies try to operate with the least amount of people needed for their normal operations, covering their extra needs through outsourcing, subcontracting, or other forms of strategic alliances with other companies. Therefore, the role of human resource planning, except in new or high growth companies, is usually limited to estimates of requirements arising from the withdrawal of persons currently employed by resignation, dismissal, or retirement.

JOB ANALYSIS

Job design is the process by which managers decide the position of each employee within the organizational structure and clarify what the employee should do in that position.

Job design should help to ensure the quality of working life and should promote good work performance. Some of the strategies that contribute to good job design are:

- Job enrichment through the delegation of authority.

- Consideration of individual differences.

- The establishment of properties that allow a positive perception of the position, including variety, significance, and autonomy.

Individual differences are particularly important in a good job design. For example, some people do better in simple routine work, while others do better in complex interesting work.

Technology is changing the work people do and their work behavior. In some ways these changes can be positive, allowing greater autonomy for the individual and also facilitating their relationships with many others inside and outside the organization, generally increasing productivity and efficiency. Among the negative aspects, there is the possibility of distractions at work as well as the dependence on prescribed systems that enforce implementing tasks automatically.

An important additional effect of technology is the possible disappearance of the concept of "job", at least in its limited sense of task or piece of work for which one is paid. Technology allows work to be structured around multiple streams of work or processes, making the rigid concept of "job" unnecessary, because people should develop various tasks and play different roles as required by these processes. The processes are displacing jobs as units of work in organizations.

OCCUPATIONAL COMPETENCIES

Competence is the quality that makes an object suitable for a certain purpose. Labor competence, in particular, is the fitness or suitability of an individual to perform a certain type of work.

The competencies are considered by some authors as personality traits and include other forms of knowledge or behavior. There has also been the intent to differentiate between skills, abilities, and competencies, and also between the potential skills and capabilities of a person and those that he actually shows at work. The only common agreement seems to be that competencies are individual characteristics that are related to the efficiency and effectiveness of a person in a particular work situation.

Trying to establish a kind of consensus on what an occupational competence is, the International Labor Organization (ILO) said: "A generally accepted concept is that competence is the effective ability to successfully perform a well-defined work activity. Occupational competence is not a success probability of executing a work; it is a real and proven ability".

Competencies management is a model or system of human capital management which is based on the analysis of the capabilities and results needed for competent performance. It is a way of aligning HRM with organizational strategy. In this model, positions and roles are designed based on the competencies required to achieve maximum performance.

There are three main techniques of evaluation or measurement of competencies: behavioral observation through simulation tests, behavioral or competency interviews, and competencies questionnaires. These techniques are applied in different phases of human resource management: selection, training and coaching, development, performance evaluation, career and succession planning, and compensation.

Although the concept of competence is widely accepted in the management of human resources, there is a discussion as to whether the potential skills and capabilities of a person are useful in predicting future performance. The general opinion seems to be cautious of potential capabilities and prefers to take into account the results obtained in previous jobs. Not only has the International Labor Organization (ILO) ruled, as we saw, that "competence is not the probability of success in the performance of a job, it is a real and proven ability", but several authors argue that the best predictor of future behavior is a person's past behavior.

RECRUITMENT AND SELECTION

Recruitment is the activity of developing a number of candidates for employment, commensurate with the human resources plan. The purpose of recruitment is to form a large enough group of candidates for managers to choose the qualified employees they need. To conduct a recruitment process, it is necessary to determine the profile or ideal attributes required in a candidate. This profile usually meets both general characteristics required of all employees of the company and specific requirements for the type of work the candidate is supposed to perform within the company.

Most companies tend to recruit the people they need through their website, newspaper ads, specialist recruitment agencies or other direct means, such as requests for information from universities or other training institutions. It is also common to allow actual employees to nominate candidates that they know and think might be suitable. This is one of the best and most economical sources of recruitment.

When required to recruit young employees, there is usually no choice but to recruit at universities or in the labor market. However, if candidates are going to occupy high or medium level positions in the organization, it is possible to recruit from within the same company. It is also possible to consider the convenience of re-hiring competent employees who have withdrawn from the company for personal, non-conflicting reasons.

In general, promotion from within the company is recommended, giving opportunities to grow to the top performers. But it is also necessary for companies to occasionally incorporate outsiders whose ability to function has been proven, especially to oc-cupy high positions in the middle layer of management. Doing so will allow the company to incorporate different ideas and work practices that contribute to a renewal of the company's way of functioning and will prevent it from becoming a closed system, isolated from the outside world.

The selection practices of an organization will determine who is hired. If conveniently designed, they will identify qualified can-didates who match the jobs and the company. The use of an ap-propriate means of selection will increase the probability of choos-ing the right person to fill a vacancy. Selection involves using ap-plications, resumes, interviews, jobs and skills tests, psychologi-cal tests, group dynamics testing, and reference checks to assess and select candidates to be presented to managers who, in the final instance, select and hire the candidates.

It is important to avoid any discrimination in the selection process. In the United States, for example, it is prohibited to ask questions about age, gender, religion, race, color, national origin, or disability in the selection process.

Perhaps the main factor to consider in selecting an employee is his achievements in previous jobs. And if the candidates have similar achievements, then it is usually preferred to choose the most intelligent.

When selecting a candidate in a modern business or any large corporation, it is necessary to take into account not only the pro-file of the individual in relation to the requirements of the immedi-ate job that is being offered, but also the individual's potential to adapt and develop within the company over time. Hiring people should be more for careers than for positions. For that reason, it is important to verify that the values of the candidate are consistent with those of the organization.

RETENTION

Suitable employee retention strategies improve organizational performance. Defining appropriate retention strategies involves identifying what motivates employees to continue working in an organization. In general, these strategies should not only include competitive wage policies but also particularly require:

- Humane treatment, with words of encouragement from managers.

- Regular information for workers about the reasons for certain decisions and the results expected of them.

- Implementing policies that demonstrate management's confidence in employees in regard to the routine activities they perform.

- Policy and organizational practices that recognize employees as friends and partners in the progress of the organization.

- Recognition and promotion policies that emphasize hard work, honesty, and integrity instead of undue favoritism.

- Benefits directly aimed at improving the welfare of the families of employees, including education, low interest loans for housing purchase, etc.

An adequate remuneration is necessary, but this is not the safest way to retain people. The most effective retention mechanisms have to do with opportunities, work environment, leadership exercised within the organization, challenges that bring out people's best capabilities, and recognition of results and performance.

Job satisfaction studies in different countries show that most employees are not happy in the organization in which they work and if they had the chance they would go to another organization. Indeed, the mobility of workers between different organizations is increasing, possibly initiated by both employees' and employers' decisions. The most important reason for leaving an organization is often a poor relationship with the boss.

FAIR DEAL AND ENFORCEMENT OF LABOR LAWS

In addition to a formal contract from a legal standpoint, when an employee enters an organization, a psychological contract between the employee and the employer is established. In general, the employer expects the worker's performance to be good and if profits are obtained as a result of the good performance, employment stability and salary increases are provided. Employees, meanwhile, expect employers to be fair with them, properly compensate their work and ensure their job security.

Apart from the formal labor contract and the psychological contract, there are laws that regulate the relations between employers and workers. Labor law is the set of principles and rules governing relations between employer(s), employee(s), trade associations, and the state.

In the legal system of each country, individual rights are established, as are the means to protect workers against employers and the state. The laws often include social rights that regulate insurable minimum guarantees for workers. Among them we can mention:

- The right to work.

- The right to minimum wage.

- Compensation for unfair dismissal.

- Working hours, weekly rest, and vacations.

- Social Security. In some countries this is a tripartite mechanism: the employee, the employer, and the state all contribute money.

- The stability of public officials.

- Health and safety, including a clean, healthy, and safe working environment. This subject includes two specific topics: accidents at work and occupational diseases.

- The right to form unions.

- The right to strike and lockout. Usually equality of arms exist: if the worker has the right to strike, the employer has the right to close. Some systems exclude the right to strike for those sectors that provide transcendental public services.

- The right to bargain collectively.

One area that is receiving increasing attention is the protection of workers against sexual or other types of harassment in the workplace (religious offenses, abuse and disrespect of women, etc.). Moreover, employers are intolerant against substance abuse at work (alcohol, drugs, etc.).

In the United States there are a number of laws to protect workers. However, the employer may terminate the employment contract at any time for any legal reason. Laws protect workers against sexual harassment or discrimination in the workplace, give them up to 12 weeks of unpaid leave per year for illness (subject to certain conditions), and establish a minimum wage and conditions for overtime pay.

PERFORMANCE EVALUATION

Performance evaluation is a comparison of what is expected of employees and their actual performance.

Although the immediate purpose of performance evaluation should be to use it as a tool to determine the actions to be executed by the employee and/or the company to improve an employee's performance, it is often used as the basis for their compensation, or more specifically, their variable compensation.

Some companies require employees to first perform a self-evaluation and then discuss it with their supervisor. In others, the supervisor directly performs the evaluation directly. Some organizations allow other people including coworkers, subordinates, or their functional supervisors to participate in the evaluation.

Performance evaluation can be based on two types of criteria, both of which are difficult to implement:

- Subjective criteria including employee behavior, willingness to collaborate with business objectives and support other employees, timeliness and effectiveness in carrying out work assignments, interest in personal development, etc. Being subjective criteria, the evaluator may have a different view of the worker's performance than the worker himself does. This difficulty has led many companies to dismiss these criteria and use more objective criteria. Others try to reduce subjectivity by involving several people in the evaluation (colleagues, subordinates, or functional supervisors of the evaluated employee).

- Objective criteria is generally the achievement of certain measurable goals. The problem is that it is very difficult to establish quantitative goals whose fulfillment depends only on the worker being evaluated. Some authors even claim that this is virtually impossible because in an organization, practically nothing can be achieved without the help of several people and it is generally very difficult to determine the degree of contribution of each of them toward the overall achievement. But despite the imprecision and possible injustice in the application of these "objective" criteria, they are used more frequently in performance evaluations.

Most performance evaluations are held once or twice a year in organizations. Several authors caution that employer feedback should be continuous and the annual performance appraisal must be simply a compendium of what the employee has heard all year. Managers should develop the good habit of giving continuous feedback to employees.

TRAINING AND WORKFORCE DEVELOPMENT

Training and development are activities in which an employee acquires more knowledge and skills that will serve to enhance their job performance. Training programs are designed to maintain or improve performance in the current job, while development programs aim to develop skills for future jobs.

A. Training

Whatever training needs are detected, the company can meet them through internal or external courses:

- Internal courses are generally taught within the premises of the company and can be delivered by experienced employees or contracted instructors. Internal courses have the advantage of reducing the cost of training and facilitate knowledge transfer within the company. Some corporations have developed it to the point that their internal training centers have become real universities, often in alliances or partnerships with traditional universities.

- External courses are academic institutions to which the company sends selected employees. External courses have the advantage of generally better quality training programs and also allow the exchange of experiences with employees of other companies, which often greatly enrich and expand the knowledge and skills of employees.

An alternative to face-to-face internal or external courses is self-training, using the computer, although some studies consider it ineffective. A better option is virtual or online education, which is spreading worldwide and whose quality is increasingly successful, representing a good opportunity to train people who travel or are unable to attend regular classroom courses.

Although companies can benefit from investing in the training of their employees, many of them invest significant amounts of money without satisfactory results. In addition to having high quality training programs, it is necessary that the activities are timely and relevant for satisfactory results to occur. Training is most effective when done at the right time to meet a specific need of an individual at work.

B. Employee Development

The development of employees within the company is not limited to training programs, but is favored by the learning opportunities and work experience within the company, especially if these opportunities have been selected according to the characteristics and specific needs of each individual.

Employee development can also be facilitated with the help of mentors. Mentors are usually employees with experience and advanced knowledge in some area, preferably occupying senior positions in the direction of an employee's career, which may help other employees to develop the skills they need to succeed in their job and the skills required for building a successful career.

COMPENSATION

Compensation is the payment of an employee in return for the work done for the company.

A. Compensation systems

Compensation or remuneration systems must be designed to attract and retain the most talented people and foster in them the best possible performance. These systems should:

- Provide financial security to employees.

- Relate their income to their productivity, their contribution to the objectives of the company, and the overall financial success of the company.

- Ensure justice and equity in wages and salaries.

- Establish special programs for executive compensation.

Most compensation systems, especially for sales people and managers include:

- A base salary in accordance with the conditions of the labor market.

- A variable salary, which is used as an incentive to reward improvements in outcomes.

The base salary must generally ensure minimum quality of life standards to the employee. The variable wage should represent a significant fraction of the total salary to constitute a real incentive to improve employee performance. In many companies, the variable remuneration of salespeople and some managers may represent several times the fixed remuneration of those employees. This variable remuneration should be linked to the fulfillment of the objectives of each employee, as measured by performance evaluation. It should be proportionate to the employee's contribution to company results and should be fair, both in terms of their contribution and in relation to the remuneration of other employees.

B. Compensation related problems

Employees do not only look at their absolute compensation, but also at the compensation received by others. They tend to be more motivated if they perceive that they are fairly paid for their contribution. However, injustices often occur in compensation systems:

- When different wages are paid to people whose contributions to the company are similar.

- When a person's work is under-rewarded.

- When a person's work is excessively rewarded. A typical example of this kind of injustice is when sales people receive a large bonus for achievements that have been possible thanks to the efforts of other people in the company who contributed directly or indirectly to enhance the sales results. Also, senior executives typically receive salaries and other privileges in excessive proportions relative to other workers.

Injustice is also often the consequence of establishing individual incentives, due to the difficulty of adequately measuring individual employee contribution to company results. Compensation based on individual incentives, although very common, is not only inconvenient for the frustration it can cause for the employees, but also because it undermines teamwork and encourages a focus on the short term. In reality, individual performance incentives decrease both the individual's and the organization's performance.

Apart from the inefficiencies and injustices of most compensation systems, when using compensation as an economic incentive to improve employee performance, it is necessary to note that even though money is always an important consideration in the minds of employees, it is never a substitute for good work relations and non-monetary recognition of the work done. Moreover, it does not matter how much a person is paid if he is subjected to abuse or misuse, required to make sacrifices that are not shared by others, or forced to pay for the strategic mistakes made by senior executives, as unfortunately occurs in many organizations.

C. Other benefits

In addition to salary compensation, companies can provide other types of benefits and services to employees to improve their quality of life and satisfaction within the company. The cost of these benefits, however, is a concern for most businesses and human resources managers worldwide.

In the United States, federal and state laws require companies to contribute to the following benefits for its employees:

- Social Security and health care (Medicare)
- Unemployment
- Compensation for workers injured on the job
- Disability insurance (some states)
- Other benefits granted by many companies include:
- Paid holidays
- Vacations
- Paid time for sickness (6-12 days a year)

- Medical insurance

- Life insurance

Other possible benefits and services include:

- Training programs and continuous development, including payment for studies at an accredited university

- Total or partial payment of transportation to and from the workplace

- Additional health benefits (drugs, dental insurance, etc.)

- Paid time off (in addition to the holidays)

- Parking facilities or parking payment for personal vehicles

- Cafeteria and food at subsidized prices

- Cultural and recreational programs

- Housing plans

- Options for company shares

- Retirement plans

The costs of employees' health benefits, welfare, and retirement are generally among those that receive more attention from human resource managers. These managers also need to consider the cost impact of labor, tax, and social consequences associated with contracted personnel or the provision of certain services by third parties.

HEALTH AND SAFETY IN THE WORK ENVIRONMENT

International conventions and the laws of many countries require the establishment of basic occupational health services, defined as preventive services, advising employers, workers, and their representatives on the requirements for establishing and maintaining a safe and healthy working environment which facilitates optimal physical and mental health in relation to work and adaptation of work to the capabilities of workers.

Health facilities at work should aim to provide workers with the tools and resources needed to create, maintain, and improve an optimal labor environment, ensuring a high level of wellness and overall health of the individual within the social context in which it operates.

All basic occupational health services should be accessible, available to any worker, able to respond to requests from interested people, capable of quality control, and should allow feedback on the process and result of the service. The different resources and tools should be kept in constant change, adapting them to the demands at the time and place that they are needed. It should be ensured that those providing the service have the ability and the capacity necessary for the performance of service and maintain regular training on each of the topics.

INDUSTRIAL RELATIONS

Labor relations include the administration and enforcement of policies and rules established by law and by the company itself, as well as the resolution of conflicts arising between the company and its employees for any breach of these provisions, the existence of a bad organizational climate, or the aspiration of higher benefits.

In some cases, these relationships take place between the company and each employee separately. However in others, labor law permits the formation of unions representing workers in a company or all workers of the same trade or industry and these unions have the right to represent their members before the company.

Collective bargaining includes all that is necessary to establish agreements or collective contracts governing the relationship between a company and the union's workers. If the union affiliates workers from several companies within the same industry, companies must unite and appoint representatives to negotiate, usually through chambers and associations. The agreements reached by these representatives will be mandatory for all companies. However, many large companies usually have internal unions and must appoint their own representatives, who must be experts in collective bargaining, to discuss and approve the required collective contracts together with the representatives of those unions.

The natural product of collective bargaining is the collective contract. This is a written summary of policies and practices which the parties have agreed in their negotiations. In general, collective agreements contain provisions for:

- Wages and salaries
- Work schedules
- Benefits and services for workers
- Privileges of union representatives
- Entitlements for the company
- Discipline
- Complaints and claims
- Promotion, termination, rehire, transfer
- Duration of the contract

Most disputes between a company and its workers are rooted in a lack of communication, the failure of collective contract compliance, or an inadequate organizational climate. Therefore, companies must ensure adequate systems, maintain channels of communication with all employees and the unions that can represent them, monitor compliance with collective agreements, and ensure continuous assessment and improvement of the organizational climate.

THE ROLE OF HUMAN RESOURCES AND BUSINESS STRATEGY

To align with the business strategy, the Human Resources (HR) function, that is the business unit responsible for the management of people, must be business-oriented.

HR should be an integral member of the management team and ensure that the culture of the organization evolves to fit with the strategy and vision of the company. However, most line managers believe that HR is not a strategic partner of the company and consider their greatest uses to consist in providing legal support, managing relationships with unions, establishing and administering benefits, and maintaining employee records.

To improve its contribution to business results, the HR function needs to:

- Increase efficiency.

- Improve its level of service.

- Focus on the core activities of the organization.

- Support organizational transformation.

- Convert human management in a core competency.

- Guide their actions by business strategy.

CHAPTER 3

ORGANIZATIONAL CHANGE

ORGANIZATIONAL CHANGE

Change is the modification or alteration of something. In particular, organizational change is the modification of one or more components of an organization: strategy, structure, systems, people, organizational skills, management style, and culture. In important changes, it is likely that if a company modifies one of these components, it will need to make adjustments to the others to maintain the necessary harmony between them.

It is important to note that for most companies it is not enough to set progressive annual goals and monitor compliance. To survive in a changing environment, a company must change. Therefore, the main reason for organizational change is to adapt or anticipate changes in the environment.

Although almost every company in the world seems to be constantly changing in order to respond to major changes in the environment, the truth is that most change efforts fail; they are too costly, too risky, or too slow. For these reasons, before any change is tried, the organization must be very sure of its need and viability. In addition, the change must be properly planned.

FACTORS AFFECTING ORGANIZATIONAL CHANGE

The drive for a company to make changes can come from many directions, which we can classify into three main categories: environment, technology, and workforce.

- *Environment.* The environment is the set of external social, cultural, economic, and political conditions in which firms operate. There is no doubt that changes in the global environment have been very significant, especially in the last two decades. The most important of these changes has been globalization. With the fall of the Soviet Union, the borders were opened to international trade and companies soon realized that the whole world could be at their reach. As a result, almost any company may act in almost any part of the world and, consequently, almost any business can be threatened by competition from any business in other region of the world. This new reality presents many opportunities but also many risks. Therefore, the greatest challenge for modern managers in companies in any country is the mental change that allows them to act with greater knowledge, courage, and security in a competitive international environment. The business environment has also become much less ethical as a result of growing greed for immediate results and short-term gains. Therefore, a difficult change is also imposed on modern management to make companies more socially responsible, acting with much greater integrity. Moreover, uncertainty and changes in the environment require companies to be more innovative as a resource to anticipate change and maintain competitiveness.

- *Technology.* Technology certainly has changed significantly. The personal computer, information and communication networks, and especially the internet have shaped a whole new world for modern business. Although companies and managers around the world have quickly grown accustomed to this change, there is still an ever pressing need in many companies to not only keep up with new technology, but to know how to use it efficiently, considering the high costs of technology investment, operation, maintenance, and updating. Moreover, despite the undoubted increase in efficiency and productivity that has been generated by new technologies, there is a serious risk of dehumanization and loss of personal contact due to the rise of email and other forms of virtual work.

- *Workforce*. Last but not least, the workforce has changed significantly in recent decades. Workers are younger, better educated, more diverse, and more technically demanding as individuals. This profound change imposes a completely different style of management. Instead of an authoritarian style of management, workers want a democratic style, one that is open to participation and promotes initiative and individual responsibility. More leaders and fewer traditional bosses are required.

CLASSIFICATION OF ORGANIZATIONAL CHANGE PROCESSES

Organizational change processes can be classified according to different criteria:

- *Depending on the purpose of the change*
  - Change of goals and strategies of the organization
  - Change of people
  - Change of products and services
  - Change in technology
  - Change in organizational structure and design
  - Change of attitudes and behaviors (culture)

- *Depending on the mode of change*
  - Imposed or facilitated change (organizational development)

- Planned or unplanned change

- Radical or incremental change

METHODS FOR CARRYING OUT ORGANIZATIONAL CHANGE

In general, there are two methods of carrying out the processes of change: imposing the change or facilitating it through organizational development.

Imposed change usually:

- Seeks to maximize shareholder value.

- Is managed top-down.

- Puts emphasis on structure and systems.

- Is guided by plans and programs.

- Is motivated by financial incentives.

- Uses consultants to analyze problems and propose solutions.

Facilitated change (organizational development) usually:

- Seeks to develop the capacity of the organization.

- Encourages bottom-up participation.

- Puts emphasis on changing behavior and employees' attitudes (culture).

- Bases the process on experiment and evolution.

- Is motivated by commitment.

- Uses consultants to support senior management in seeking their own solutions.

Although change must sometimes be imposed, for example to comply with new regulations, and in almost all significant organizational changes there is often some degree of enforcing, it is generally preferable to facilitate change, promoting and supporting employee participation in the process.

PLANNED ORGANIZATIONAL CHANGE

Facilitated or planned change, usually called organizational development, is the set of actions within an organization that increase its effectiveness. It involves the intervention of consultants or advisors, usually external, who are also called change agents. The role of these advisers is essentially to help the organization to learn.

Many of the ideas on organizational development presented in this chapter are due to the work of Professor Thomas Cummings of the University of Southern California, and Professor Christopher Worley of Pepperdine University.

Planned organizational change attempts to modify the design and processes of an organization to make it more effective and efficient and involves a number of activities that can be summarized as follows:

- Entry and contracting
- Diagnosis
- Planning and implementing change
- Evaluation and institutionalization of change

ENTRY AND CONTRACTING

The process of organizational development generally begins when a representative from a company contacts a professional or a consulting firm to help solve a problem.

When contacted, the consultant or professional organizational development specialist should work with the person that has requested his services to properly define the problem and establish the relevant counterparts within the company to undertake the solution. Then the consultant will present the client with a proposal to help solve the problem. The proposal should include the following elements:

- Definition of the problem

- Objectives of the change process

- Change strategy

- Change management plan

- Identification of responsibilities

- Budget

Following submission of the proposal, the consultant and the client shall provide mutual expectations, negotiate the time and resources, and establish the basic rules to collaborate and work together. They will then use these to create a contract that will govern relations between the parties.

DIAGNOSIS OF AN ORGANIZATION

Diagnosis is the identification of the nature of a problem in an organization through the observation of characteristic signs and symptoms, as well as the collection, processing, and analysis of available relevant information.

The diagnosis should aim to:

- Understand and validate problems and needs.

- Identify strengths and supports.

- Define responsibilities and commitments.

There are different models for performing the diagnosis of an organization. Most of them involve three levels of analysis: organizational, group, and individual. For each level, the entries or information needs, design components, and outputs or products of analysis must be defined. The goal of diagnosis is to determine the effectiveness and efficiency of the organization in general, but also of its teams and individuals.

The main data collection methods for the diagnosis of an organization are:

- Personal interviews

- Questionnaires

- Observation

- Secondary sources

The main techniques for analyzing the data collected for the diagnosis of an organization are:

- Qualitative techniques (content analysis, force field analysis)

- Quantitative techniques (average, standard deviation, and frequency distribution; dispersion diagrams and correlation coefficients; tests of differences)

After performing the diagnosis of an organization, one of these two procedures can be used for feedback:

- The consultant makes a summary of the information obtained from the questionnaires and this summary is discussed in a working group of the organization. This is known as a "feedback survey ".

- The senior management of the company evaluates its own performance before doing the same at lower levels. This is known as "survey-guided development"

CHANGE MANAGEMENT

There are alternative approaches for managing change:

- Management of change through power

- Managing change through reason

- Managing change through reeducation

In many cases it will be necessary to use all three types of these approaches to achieve the desired change results.

To facilitate the change process, it is desirable to use any of the various change management models available. Perhaps the first proposed change model was one developed shortly after World War II by Kurt Lewin, a German-American psychologist considered one of the pioneers of social, organizational, and applied psychology . The Lewin change model is based on increasing the forces that try to bring about change and reduce or neutralize the forces that try to maintain the current status. Lewin suggests three steps to this process:

- *Defrost*. Provide information on the need for change and mitigate the forces trying to keep the current state.

- *Move or change*. Act on the organization to bring about change.

- *Refreeze*. Stabilize the organization to another level of equilibrium

A more recent model, proposed by Professor John Kotter, from Harvard University, suggests that the following steps be taken to transform an organization:

- Establish a sense of urgency to change

- Form a powerful conductive coalition

- Create a vision

- Communicate that vision

- Empower others to act on that vision and remove barriers to the change process

- Plan and create short-term wins in the desired direction

- Consolidate improvements and produce more change

- Institutionalize the changes in the culture of the organization

Interestingly, both models are highly political. The authors did not use any reference to politics to present and disseminate their models of change, but recognized the existence of opposing forces within organizations and in the case of the model proposed by Kotter, it very accurately describes the process that usually takes out a political leader when he wants to promote a change in his country or community.

Important processes of change must be led by the highest executive authority of the organization and this individual generally bears the responsibility for the success of the process. The experience of leading successful organizational change processes suggests that they should:

- Relate the change with the mission and values of the organization.

- Invest a great deal in building skills.

- Leverage peer pressure (ensuring that they influence each other).

- Create social support (ensuring that leaders become instructors).

- Align rewards and ensure accountability.

- Change the environment (change the processes, structure, etc.).

Leaders of change must lead by example and act with great persistence to achieve their objective.

RESISTANCE TO CHANGE

Perhaps individual differences are manifested with greater intensity in the process of change. People react differently to changes; sometimes they are not easy to digest. With any change, some accept it or are indifferent, but others resist actively or passively.

In almost all processes of change, resistance of at least one part of the organization manifests. Often this resistance is due to the lack of knowledge about the need and purpose of change, lack of participation in the process, fear of the consequences of change, or a combination of these factors.

To overcome resistance to change, Professor Kotter, mentioned above, suggests the following actions:

- Educating and communicating (about change)

- Engaging and involving

- Facilitating and supporting

- Negotiating and agreeing

- Manipulating and co-opting (for example, giving an individual an attractive role in the change process)

- Coercing (explicitly or implicitly)

The process of change must take into account the culture of the organization. Culture is the set of beliefs that people in an organization have invented, discovered, or developed. Culture is based on a social learning process and can't be changed without creating a lot of anxiety in the organization. The change process should provide the adapting effort the organization needs in order to take in a cultural change.

The influence of culture in the process of change becomes particularly difficult in global companies. Interventions that work in one country may not work in others. To avoid failure in these efforts for change, cultural diversity must be taken into account, allowing different countries to carry out the change process, with the consideration of each country's cultural specificity. As far as possible, the desired change should be compatible with all the different cultures involved.

ORGANIZATIONAL DEVELOPMENT INTERVENTIONS

Organizational development interventions are the set of actions that are performed in different areas of the company in order to help improve performance and efficiency.

The design of interventions involves:

- Determining the degree of choice that the company has regarding the change.

- Determining what needs to be changed.

- Determining where the consultant or agent of change should begin to intervene.

- Making a choice of technologies and methodologies of intervention.

For interventions to be effective, employees must have been previously convinced of the need for change.

Employees are more actively involved in the change process if they:

- Understand and share the reasons for change.

- Are able to learn new ways of acting and working.

- Are involved in change projects.

- Feel that their needs are met, have confidence in the company, and are happy with their work

Interventions can be classified according to their object:

- Interventions in the human process (coaching, training and development)

- Interventions in structure and work processes (structure design, restructuring, reengineering)

- Interventions in human resource management (performance management, development and help for employees)

- Strategic interventions (strategic change, mergers and acquisitions, alliances)

- Organizational development interventions tend to focus on people (human processes and human resource management).

INTERVENTION IN HUMAN PROCESSES

Change programs can be applied to:

- Individuals

- Interpersonal relationships

- Group dynamics

Individual approaches may include:

- Coaching (advice to facilitate individual learning)

- Training and development (traditional school methods; on-the-job training (OJT)

- Interpersonal and group approaches may include:

- Process consulting

- Third-party interventions (for management and resolution of conflicts)

- Team building

At the organizational level, the following approaches may be used to improve performance and labor relations:

- Working groups (to solve problems)

- Intergroup intervention (to improve relations between groups or departments)

- Intervention in large groups (to present a new vision or resolve urgent problems)

INTERVENTION IN HUMAN RESOURCE MANAGEMENT

Although interventions can occur in all phases of human resource management in important change processes, usually the most frequent interventions are in performance management and the training and development of employees.

Intervention in performance management seeks to improve the efficiency of this process and align it with the objectives of change, ensuring that:

- Managers and employees work together to set specific and measurable goals.

- A good feedback system that checks whether the goals were achieved is established.

- Incentives to improve performance of employees and working groups are defined.

The development of employees is designed to help them learn to do their job more effectively and also enhance their skills and their potential to become agents of change. Employee development includes:

- Career planning

- Career development

- Diversity management

- Intervention in employee stress and well-being

EVALUATION OF CHANGE

The assessment of change is the set of activities that determines whether the objectives of the change process are being achieved.

Evaluations can be performed during the intervention, immediately after its conclusion, or at a later time.

INSTITUTIONALIZING CHANGE

Change is permanent when it becomes institutional, when it is part of the culture and the way things are done in an organization.

To institutionalize change, it is necessary to:

- Show people how the new approaches, behaviors, and attitudes have helped to improve performance.

- Allow sufficient time to ensure that the new generation of senior managers personifies the new approach.

INNOVATION

Many companies want to be innovative, meaning they want to be able to make significant changes in the market. But to be innovative, they must start making major changes within themselves, in their components, and, above all, in their culture.

The innovativeness of a company depends on the existence of:

- Adequate resources and skills to innovate.

- Market orientation.

- Effective leadership.

- The free exchange of ideas.

- An environment that enables change.

- Research and development.

Innovation studies have shown that:

- Creativity precedes innovation. Creativity refers to the generation of ideas and innovation refers to the transformation of these ideas into new products, services or markets.

- Innovation is a slow process. Innovation is not born as a result of haste, it is born as a result of effort, perseverance, method, dedication, a certain amount of patience, and, above all, the exchange of ideas and knowledge.

- Innovation is a task of the whole company. Innovation cannot simply be a task of research and development teams, but must encompass the management and all other members of the organization in an environment where imagination and initiative are promoted.

- It is not easy to measure innovation. The most common measure is the percentage of sales generated by new products, but this measure reflects only one aspect of innovation in the company.

- Innovation is highly beneficial to the company. Innovation promotes competition, growth and market share, financial performance, and the survival of the company.

CHAPTER 4

LEADERSHIP DEVELOPMENT

CONCEPT OF LEADERSHIP

Dictionaries define leadership as the position of a leader of a group, organization, etc. According to this interpretation, leadership in a company is associated with people in higher positions, and among them is the Chief Executive Officer (CEO). However, it may occur that a person who occupies the highest position does not have leadership and, conversely, a person who does not occupy the top position in an organization can be the most important leader within it.

Leadership can then be best understood as the power or ability to lead other people or, maybe better, as the process of a leader's influence over his followers to bring about a change. The following are the components of this last definition:

- Leadership is a relationship between a leader and his followers. "A leader is someone who has followers" said Peter Drucker, a well- known consultant and author of management books in the last century. Indeed, one cannot imagine a leader without followers.

- The relationship between a leader and his followers is one of influence. A true leader is voluntarily followed by his followers. Therefore, the relationship between a leader and followers is not a relationship of authority or subordination but of influence or prestige. Often the followers also influence the leader, but in general, it is the leader who exerts a greater influence on the relationship.

- Leadership is intended to bring about change. A leader has followers because they are all interested in modifying or improving the situation in which they find themselves and need a guide who conducts the necessary process of change. Otherwise, those followers would not need a leader.

DISTINCTION BETWEEN LEADERSHIP AND MANAGEMENT

One important thing to keep in mind is the difference between leadership and management. Some authors, among them professor John Kotter of Harvard University, believe that management has to do with administration and the maintenance of order in a company, while leadership is about coping with change. The manager plans, develops, and administers a budget; organizes and assigns staff; and monitors and resolves problems, while the leader sets a direction and aligns and motivates people.

This distinction, although correct, can lead to confusion. It could be understood that a business needs a set of leaders at the highest levels of the hierarchy and a set of managers at the middle levels, each set performing different functions. Actually, although leadership and management are different functions, leaders and managers should not be two different people. Indeed, the strategy can't be separated from the execution. All managers and even most (if not all) employees in the organization must also be leaders. They should be involved in strategy formation and must possess the ability to influence others to do the right things.

Managers can't be successful without being good leaders, and leaders can't be successful without being good managers. Of course, the demands of leadership should be higher for senior executives.

LACK OF LEADERSHIP

Despite the importance of leadership in any organization, particularly at the highest levels, weakness and/or a lack of leadership is often observed. A common manifestation of the lack of leadership is the misuse of authority by many managers trying to use their formal authority without first earning the respect of the people or modeling behavior and accomplishments without proper actions. Unfortunately the great majority of managers in many companies who act that way get only resistance from their subordinates, rather than cooperation. Hence the extraordinary interest in understanding the nature of leadership and finding ways to develop the leaders that organizations need.

ROLE OF A LEADER

As mentioned, the role or mission of the leader is to promote and achieve the desired change for himself and his followers.

To carry out their mission effectively, a leader must:

- Interpret the situation in which they find change necessary and display the direction of the needed change.

- Take responsibility for guiding their followers in the change process.

- Create a culture that is favorable to change.

- Respond to the reality of the diverse environment that characterizes modern organizations.

- Act as mentors and facilitators of people in change processes.

Leaders must learn to create an environment that can adopt the change not as a threat, but as an opportunity. That is the only way an organization can be run in a turbulent world.

In leading a project of major change, it is important for leaders to recognize that the process of change must be developed in stages and that each stage is important and may require a significant amount of time. Leaders are responsible for guiding the organization and employees through the change process.

TRANSFORMATIONAL LEADERSHIP

Although all leadership is related to change, the terms strategic leadership and transformational leadership have been proposed to identify change leadership more precisely. Of these two terms, transformational leadership is currently the most widely accepted. Transformational leadership is understood as the ability of a leader to cause significant changes in both followers and the organization.

A concept that is often associated with transformational leadership is charismatic leadership. Charismatic leadership has been defined as a type of leadership in which the leader generates enthusiasm and motivates followers through inspiration, example, intellectual stimulation, and individual consideration.

Proponents of the concept of transformational leadership have included charisma as a fundamental characteristic or component. For these authors, the ability of a leader to bring about significant changes in their followers depends on their ability to excite, inspire, and motivate them. However, not everyone agrees with this idea. Charisma can be used to manipulate followers, and indeed it has been (the case of Adolf Hitler is a significant example).For this reason, some think that trust is what should prevail in the relationship between leader and followers, not charisma.

THEORIES OF LEADERSHIP

The main traditional paradigms of leadership theory are:

- *Theories of traits.* These are used to explain the personal characteristics of effective leaders.

- *Theories of behavior.* These aim to understand what leaders do.

- *Contingency theories.* The purpose of these traits is to determine which leadership style is most appropriate based on the leader, the followers, and the situation.

Recently there have been new approaches or theories that are more interested in the leader's relationship with followers than in the leader himself. These approaches include that of transformational leadership, which we have discussed.

THEORIES OF LEADERSHIP TRAITS

Theories of leadership traits attempt to identify the distinctive personal features that explain leadership effectiveness. The proposed features can be classified into the following groups:

- *Personality traits* (extroversion, emotional stability, desire to be a leader, energy, confidence, intelligence)

- *Traits of humanity* (kindness, sensitivity to others)

- *Performance traits* (vision, openness to experience, willingness to take responsibility, integrity, flexibility)

Different authors that have addressed the issue of leadership do not agree on what the most important features or attributes of a leader are, although the vision, emotional and social intelligence, and values seem to stand out from these features:

- *Vision*. Vision is generally considered the main attribute of a leader. The leader must be able to envision a desired situation and clearly express that vision. They must live that dream or vision and turn it into something real for an organization.

- *Emotional Intelligence*. The leader must possess a high degree of "emotional intelligence", the ability to manage emotions. Successful leaders show deep sympathy and empathy, which is an intellectual or emotional identification with another; understanding, or mutual affection; ability to share ideas and emotions of another; and concern or interest in others.

- *Values.* In addition to vision and ability to manage emotions and relationships with others, leaders must have values. Values are the fundamental beliefs that an individual thinks are important. Higher values are justice, fairness, respect, integrity, and courage. Courage in particular has been recognized as a fundamental value for moral leadership. Courage means accepting responsibility, showing dissatisfaction, taking risks, asking for what you want, saying what you think, and fighting for what you believe in.

These attributes are often added to many others, which makes it very difficult to be a leader, and judging by the dearth of leaders frequently referenced in all areas, maybe it is. But we must realize that no leader is perfect. No leader should pretend to be perfect, but should instead focus on using his strengths to see that others supplement his weaknesses or limitations.

Theories of leadership traits are obsolete. Many leaders do not have all the features that they are supposed to possess according to these theories. And what's more, many people who are not leaders possess those features, making it very difficult to predict the leadership potential of a person judging by the given criteria. For example, many people have emotional and social intelligence or practice core values but they are not leaders. There are people that have a sense of vision, but they are not leaders. Although certain personality traits and skills indicate a greater likelihood of success in a leadership role, they alone are not sufficient to ensure effective leadership.

THEORIES OF LEADERSHIP BEHAVIOR

Instead of looking at the personality traits of a leader, theories of leadership behavior try to understand what a leader does. In particular, these theories try to describe the behaviors that distinguish effective leaders.

The proper behavior of a leader, as most of these theories have found, should include a willingness and ability to:

- *Motivate.* The motivation of the other begins with the motivation of the leader himself. The leader must be able to arouse enthusiasm in his people in order for their motivation and performance to markedly improve.

- *Empower.* To motivate their followers, the leader's behavior should not only serve as a model, but should be based on the empowerment of the followers.

- *Create a good working environment.* Rather than control the work of others, the job of the leader is to promote a motivating work environment. This task includes setting clear performance expectations, removing obstacles, and using rewards and discipline appropriately.

Behavioral theories and theories of leadership traits have received similar criticism. That is, some leaders adopt behaviors that are considered appropriate for a good leader and others do not, while remaining effective as leaders. Moreover, some people adopt behaviors that should make them leaders according to the theories of behavior, but it does not happen that way. It is possible that these forms of behavior make them good people and even good managers or supervisors, but not necessarily leaders.

CONTINGENCY THEORY OF LEADERSHIP

The contingency approach, which could be considered as a variant of the behavioral approach, is based on the assumption that the most appropriate leadership style depends on the circumstances.

Contingency leadership theories try to determine which leadership style is most suitable, according to the characteristics of the leader, the followers, and the situation.

Style is a characteristic mode or form of acting or being. Overall, four leadership styles are distinguished:

- *Autocratic*. The leader exercises authority over followers.

- *Supportive*. The leader provides advice and guidance to followers.

- *Participative or democratic*. The leader promotes the involvement of supporters in decision making.

- *Achievement oriented*. The leader sets goals and expects followers to strive to achieve them.

Other criteria have been proposed to classify leadership styles. For example, leadership focused on the task or leadership focused on the relationship with the people involved.

Contingency leadership theories are based on the concept of situational leadership. Situational leadership, in turn, is based on the conviction that the most appropriate leadership style depends on the situation. This approach assumes that no single leadership style is the best in all circumstances.

The main situational leadership models that have been proposed include the following:

- Fiedler's Leadership Contingency model. Fiedler affirms that group performance depends on the interaction between the style of leadership and the nature of the situation. His theory is based on defining when a task-oriented style or a relationship-oriented style is most appropriate according to the situation.

- Vroom-Yetton-Jago model. No leadership style alone is appropriate; the leader must be flexible enough to change leadership styles (autocratic, consultative, and participatory) and adjust to specific situations.

- House's model of Path-Goal Leadership. According to this model, leaders are efficient because of their positive effect on the motivation, ability to execute, and satisfaction of their followers. The theory is called path-goal because it focuses on how the leader influences the followers' perception of work goals and personal development and the routes to reach them. The type of leader behavior depends, in this case, on the personal characteristics of group members and the work environment.

- The Hersey-Blanchard Situational Leadership model. The leader must apply the leadership style most appropriate to the maturity level of his followers.

The contingency theories of leadership have also been heavily criticized. Some authors claim that leadership style is associated with the personality of an individual and since the latter is relatively stable, it is not easy to change leadership style. Others think that management style is an aspect of form, and therefore is not as important; what really matters is the leader's competence in accomplishing his mission.

Instead of proposing a change of leadership style according to the situation, as situational leadership does, critics of this approach argue that it is preferable to seek the most appropriate leader for each situation. This is possibly what has happened throughout history, in different fields of human activity. Churchill, for example, was a very appropriate leader to direct the resistance of England and its allies during World War II, but was not considered by the British people to be the right leader after the war.

LEADERSHIP COMPETENCIES

From the point of view of the development of future leaders, the competencies approach seems more useful than the approaches or theories of traits, behavior, and contingency. In a way, the competencies approach can integrate the different theories of leadership.

Leadership competencies are a person's skills and fitness to be an effective leader. A review of the literature on leadership, including its relevant theories, allows us to identify the core competencies that a leader should possess:

- Commitment to service. A true leader should not seek fame or prestige, but the success of his followers.

- Strategic thinking. To fulfill their mission, a leader must be able to formulate and implement the necessary strategy.

- Experience and knowledge. A leader must possess the experience and knowledge necessary to perform his mission and inspire confidence in their followers.

- The ability to acquire and use power. A leader must know how to acquire and use power to fulfill their mission.

- The ability to act according to the situation. A leader must know how to interpret the situation and act in the most convenient manner.

- Personality traits. A leader must possess certain personality traits that can help him to fulfill his mission, especially intelligence, self-esteem, and courage.

- Ability to establish an effective relationship with followers. A leader must be able to establish an effective relationship with his followers to make an impact or transformation in them so he can accomplish his mission.

- Proper handling of emotions. Proper management of emotions is necessary for anyone, but much more so for a leader.

LEADERSHIP OF ORGANIZATIONS

The leader of an organization is one who communicates their ideas and wins acceptance of them from members of the organization, making these members his followers and encouraging them to support and implement the ideas through change.

To be a leader of an organization, a person needs to have power within it: formal power, personal power, or preferably both. Those who want to be leaders of an organization must do what is necessary to win their power and use it in order to get the results they want for the organization.

GLOBAL ORGANIZATIONAL LEADERSHIP

The new realities of today's world require that the leaders of global organizations not only have general leadership competencies, but also possess the following skills or abilities:

- The ability to manage complexity. Today's world, particularly with regard to the activity of global companies, is difficult and complicated because it is formed by a large number of intertwined elements due to globalization among other factors. The leaders of global organizations must be able to understand this complexity and act effectively within it.

- Cross-cultural competence. The most important competence that a leader of a global organization must have is the ability to develop relationships with people from different cultures. The leaders of global organizations face a number of dilemmas, usually due to the need to establish rules of universal application, yet they treat every culture as a special case of diversity. Cross-cultural competence has been defined as the ability to integrate seemingly opposing values.

- The ability to lead virtual teams. The modern workplace, especially in global organizations, is largely based on virtual teams and the leader of these organizations should be able to properly address them. The appropriate use of technology for communication and tracking team progress are key factors to the success of virtual leaders.

RELATIONSHIP BETWEEN LEADER AND FOLLOWERS

Leadership, as we have defined it, is a voluntary relationship between followers and the leader. Leadership is not just an individual phenomenon. Leadership is impossible without followers. No change can occur without motivated and committed followers.

To forge a good relationship with their followers, leaders must:

- Recognize and appreciate the work of their followers.

- Remind people of what is important.

- Build and maintain trust.

- Establish intimate alliances with their followers.

The essence of leadership is trust. It is impossible to lead people who do not trust you. The only way to exercise leadership is through informal authority, convincing people to do what you want them to do.

A leader's vision must be shared by their followers. A shared vision builds trust among followers, encourages people to try to make that vision a reality, and creates a work environment in which decisions are made more easily and quickly because it is clear to everyone how every decision fits into the big picture.

The relationship between leader and followers is a relationship of influence. In order to earn this relationship, the leader, according to Robert B. Cialdini of Arizona State University, has to:

- Make his followers see him as a friend, appearing to like them and speak well of them.

- Display interest in his followers and try to favor them. The followers then feel obliged to return these favors.

- Show his followers the behavior to be followed and make them see that the majority behave that way.

- Ensure that his followers are committed to him or his ideas. Once they are, followers will try to remain consistent with their commitment.

- Teach his followers that he is in charge; he has the information and the power.

- Convince his followers that by following him, they will have more of what they lack most.

The relationship between followers and the leader is very rarely permanent. Generally, this relationship is circumstantial, depending on the existence of conditions that favor the relationship. Organizations in particular do not always have the same leader. The responsibility of leadership is often taken in turns and is widely shared as organizations develop over time. In addition, all leaders are followers at times.

If a leader tries to treat all of his followers alike, they are very unlikely to succeed. Dyadic theory is an approach to leadership that tries to explain why leaders vary their behavior with different followers. Overall, this theory suggests that leaders often divide their followers into two groups: included (near the leader) and excluded (far from him). This distinction between included and excluded depends on the size and geographic distribution of the group of followers, the leader's characteristics, the behavior of the follower, etc. Modern technology (television, the internet, social networks, etc.) facilitates leader contact with his followers, even over long distances, which can allow many followers to feel included, but such media is not a replacement for effective personal contact that can generate greater confidence in the relationship between leader and followers.

DEVELOPMENT OF FOLLOWERS

The leader of an organization must be a leader of leaders, so his main job is to actively help their followers to achieve their full leadership potential. The leader must surround them with good people, help them learn, and stimulate their growth and development.

The leader has the duty and the need to ensure the development of their followers. Developing others involves genuine and continued willingness to promote learning and skills development in those people.

To help develop their followers, a leader must possess and strengthen his skills of:

- Communication
- Coaching

- Conflict management

A. Communication

Leadership involves effective interpersonal communication and is based not so much on good speaking and writing, despite its importance, but on knowing how to listen: seeking first to understand, then to be understood.

The leader must practice support communication, seeking to preserve a positive relationship with followers at the time that they are communicating.

The leader must make use of feedback to help individuals and organizations learn and improve. He must also create the conditions for open communication, ensuring that all information is shared in the organization, especially across functional and hierarchical boundaries.

A leader's communication skills are especially important during times of rapid change, uncertainty, or crisis. In times of crisis it is important that leaders:

- Remain calm and sharpen their listening skills.

- Are visible.

- Tell the truth.

- Communicate a vision for the future.

In their relationship with other people, the leader must be able to serve as a model for the person he hopes to turn into his follower. This relationship usually involves personal counseling of the followers, conveying advice and information and setting standards for them.

B. Coaching

Personal counseling does not necessarily mean teaching someone else. Often, it simply means helping others to recognize and use their own capabilities to become their own leaders.

C. Conflict management

Interpersonal relationships often lead to the existence of conflicts. It is the duty of a leader to properly handle disputes among his followers as well as his own conflicts with his followers and with other leaders.

LEADERSHIP OF TEAMS

The team leader should be a coach. His capacity is based on his ability to leverage and enhance the work of the team. Teamwork means that all members of a team focus on a common purpose and the climate of the team is one of trust, respect, open communication, and cooperation.

A. Team effectiveness

To ensure the effectiveness of the team, the leader must:

- Develop team cohesion through interaction and agreement on a mission and shared goals.

- Ensure an appropriate balance between the task and the socio-emotional needs of team members.

- Exercise a personal impact through recognizing the importance of purpose and shared values, admitting their own mistakes, and supporting and coaching team members.

B. Special teams

Virtual teams and global teams pose special leadership challenges and require effective use of information technology to facilitate the participation of team members and the ability to widely share information.

Another special type of team is that of self-led teams. These are characterized by relative autonomy and because its members share or rotate through leadership positions, they are mutually responsible for a set of performance goals assigned by senior management. Self-led teams can be very effective, but require top management to appoint those who are able to work together without direct managerial oversight, give them clear goals, and provide them with the resources needed to achieve those goals.

C. Effective meetings

Working in teams usually requires regular meetings with different purposes and participants. Meetings are very important to ensure communication and the distribution of information, but they must be efficient in order to fulfill their function. The efficiency of meetings depends on planning, management, and monitoring.

To achieve effective meetings, the leader must:

- Determine the purpose and need for the meeting.

- Establish what specific problem is to be considered, what the facts about this problem are, and what the possible solutions and their consequences will be.

- Define the right time and place for the meeting and ensure a physical environment conducive to a successful meeting.

- Allow participants to get to know each other if they have not previously met.

- Ensure that the meeting is as brief as the subject or subjects to be discussed permit.

- Provide that all attendees participate, no one monopolizes the discussion, the discussion focuses on the agenda, decisions are made by consensus, and the objectives of the meeting are achieved.

- Ensure the meeting ends with an evaluation of its results and there is a clear definition of further actions required and the people responsible for these actions.

- Ensure and verify that the actions agreed at the meeting are conducted.

LEADERSHIP DEVELOPMENT

To become a leader, a person must:

- Build an inner excellence by mastering the context of his own life, knowing himself, being optimistic and enthusiastic, and remaining calm when solving problems.

- Act as a leader by caring for people, innovating and creating a compelling vision that will lead people to a new level, building trust by acting with integrity, forging alliances, and having faith in people and teamwork.

- Acquire leadership experience by assuming progressive management responsibilities and improving the ability to influence people and exert greater impact on the organization.

The person who aspires to be a leader should make special efforts to develop general leadership skills: commitment to service, strategic thinking, experience and knowledge, a capacity to acquire and use power, an ability to act according to the situation, self-esteem and courage, an ability to establish an effective relationship with his followers, and proper management of emotions.

One way to develop leadership in an organization is to create opportunities to enable young people to take leadership responsibilities and train them in team management. It is also necessary to provide them with role models and allow them to make mistakes as part of their learning process.

CHAPTER 5

MANAGERIAL COMMUNICATION

THE CONCEPT AND IMPORTANCE OF MANAGERIAL COMMUNICATION

Communication is the process of dealing with someone verbally or in writing. Communication is important for managers for the following reasons:

- Communication is the process of linking the various management functions (it is at the heart of all organizations).

- Communication is the primary means by which people obtain and share information.

- Managers spend most of their time communicating with employees, colleagues, clients, and others.

- Information and communication are sources of power in organizations.

Effective communication allows managers to achieve their business goals. Communication is effective when it adequately conveys what the manager intends to transmit and creates desired changes or positive reactions in the receiver.

Improving the communication skills of a manager involves developing their assertiveness. An assertive person can communicate with people at all levels in an open, direct, frank, and appropriate manner. Among the factors that could have a positive effect on the development of self-esteem are affection, love, and acceptance.

COMMUNICATION STRATEGY

Strategy is the set of activities designed to achieve a goal. According to Professor Mary Munter of Dartmouth, we can distinguish five components or variables in interactive communication strategy:

- The communicator. The communicator (writer or speaker) must be clear about the objective pursued, choose an appropriate style for communication, and ensure their credibility with the audience.

- The audience. To communicate effectively, you must know who makes up the audience, what they know and expect, how they feel, and how they can be persuaded .

- The message. The message should emphasize the conclusion from the beginning. Ideas should be organized according to the objective pursued.

- The channel. The channel is the means by which the message is transmitted: written channels, voice channels, or mixed channels. Proper selection of the channel is also an important decision to the communication strategy.

- The context. Communication must take into account the cultural characteristics of the audience (political, social, etc.) and their preferences of communication style and channel.

WRITTEN COMMUNICATION: ADVANTAGES AND DISADVANTAGES

Written communication has the following advantages:

- It provides a record for reference and follow-up.

- It allows economical communication of a single message to many people.

- But written communication has at least two disadvantages:

- The sender does not know whether the communication was received, unless the recipient acknowledges receipt .

- Anyone can become upset if he perceives that any data, information, or opinion presented in a document would harm him and/or may be misinterpreted by someone else who reads it.

WRITTEN COMMUNICATION: COMPOSITION

A composition is a text prepared for printing or transmission. Before writing, it is important that the author revises and keeps his communication strategy in mind.

Any composition consists of three main parts:

- The beginning or introduction. The beginning (the title and the first paragraph) must be attractive.

- The body. Maintaining order in the composition is very important.

- The end or conclusion. One should take care to close the document with an effective sentence that leaves a deep impression on the reader.

One of the most important objectives of composition is to achieve clarity in writing. Clarity is the ease with which ideas are expressed in the document. To ensure clarity of a text, one must take into account:

- *Unity*. In a document made of several parts, unity comes from the relationship of the various elements with the theme or central idea. So anything that has no connection with the purpose of the document must be discarded.

- *Coherence*. Ideas should be developed in an appropriate order.

- *Emphasis*. The document should fix the reader's attention on what matters most. Emphasis is embodied through the space allocated to each part, the location itself, and through repetition.

WRITTEN COMMUNICATION: STYLE

Style is one's way of saying something. The style of a document should be appropriate for the type and nature of the document. The writer's choice involves deciding on the degree of formality desired, the appropriate use of words and phrases, and the use of technical or specialized terms.

Style is the soul, the personality of the writing. The main style rules are:

- Simplicity. To achieve one needs to keep focus on the issue, avoid the unnecessary, put "one thing after another ", and use direct forms.

- Concrete, normal, and precise vocabulary.

- The rhythm of exposure. The writer must use punctuation in correspondence with the movement of the discourse and make the breaks that are considered essential.

- Brevity. Eliminate any unnecessary words and restrict the message to what is essentially significant.

WRITTEN COMMUNICATION: APA STANDARDS

The standards of the American Psychological Association (APA) aim to facilitate the proper use of sources and references needed to produce a document, giving due credit to these sources and avoiding plagiarism. Although the use of these standards is mandatory in academic or research papers, they can be used in any type of professional or managerial document.

The APA standards regulate, in general, the way that the references are cited in a document and how they are written and arranged in a list at the end of the document.

All ideas that are taken from a reference when writing a document should be cited therein. Aside from allowing credit to the sources being used, citing references also allows to provide quick information from books, journals, or internet sites that were consulted to support the ideas in the development of a work. Some of the key standards in terms of citations of references are:

- When a reference is cited in the text or body of work, it is sufficient to indicate as follows: Author's surname (Year). The reader, if he desires, could then go to the list of references at the end of the document and find more complete information on this topic.

- If you copy verbatim in a sentence, it must be placed in quotation marks and the citation should include the page number on which that phrase is found in the cited reference. If the quotation has more than 40 words, it should be written as a separate paragraph, omitting quotation marks.

- All references cited in the text or body of the document must be written in a list at the end of the document. Any reference that has not been cited in the text should not appear in this list. Some of the major standards for the list of references are:

- The list of references should be ordered alphabetically by surname of the authors, indicating the following information: Author's surname, Author's name initials (Year of publication), Title of document, Publisher (editorial, journal), or Website.

- When the reference is an article published in a journal, the number of the journal and of the pages on which the article appears should be added. When it comes to a document or information taken from a website, the date on which the information was recovered should be indicated, since the content of the site can be changed and the information may no longer be available on the site.

WRITTEN COMMUNICATION: GRAMMAR

Grammar is the set of rules that are set for the correct use of a language. Below are some of the most important grammar rules for the English language.

A. Sentences

Sentences should have this structure:

Subject (initiates the sentence) + Verb (establishes a situation) + Complement (completes the verbal idea) + Modifier (adds information: time, place)

Example: A farmer grows tomatoes in a garden.

B. Commas

Commas are used for connecting two ideas in a single sentence.

Example: He left in a hurry, and in danger.

Commas are also used to separate units in a list.

Example: There were cows, dogs, and cats.

C. Semicolon

A semicolon is used to join two ideas.

Example: Some people prefer money; others prefer recognition.

- *Present tense*

The present tense is used:

- To express a future idea. Example: She goes to the airport tomorrow.

- General truth. Example: Babies cry.

- Habitual or regular action. Example: I eat everyday.

- Ability. Example: I cook.

- Immediate sensory perceptions. Example: I want more.

- *Past tense*

  The past tense is used in:

  - Finished or terminated actions. Example: He left.

  - Conditional sentences. Example: He would help you if he knew where you were.

  - Sequence of tenses. Example: He said he wanted to live.

  The past tense is formed in different ways:

  - The addition of ed (regular verbs)

  - The dictionary form in the verbs: cut, set, cost, hit, put, hurt, let

  - Internal changes (irregular verbs)

D. Pronouns

A pronoun is a word that takes the place of a noun. Pronouns can be used in one of three cases:

1. Subject. Example: He did the job. (He is the pronoun in this case.)

2. Object. Example: Jim talked to him. (Him is the pronoun in this case.)

3. Possessive. Example: The stock price reaches its highest level. (Its is the pronoun in this case.)

BEST ADVICE FOR NEW WRITERS

The best advice for those who want to write well, according to the great writers, is to just write. You learn to write correctly and effectively by writing often and trying to improve your design, clarity, style, and all other attributes of your writing.

BUSINESS PRESENTATIONS

We can distinguish several types of business presentations according to their objective:

- Information
- Sales
- Discussion

All presentations must be carefully prepared to ensure that they adequately convey the intended message. The speaker should also maintain control of the audience at all times during the presentation.

Although it us usual in business presentations to utilize visual aids, they do not always have to be used. They should be used if the message is difficult to convey without them or if the speaker does not have good memory or practice with the subject material, needing the visual aids to make sure he is not forgetting something important or to maintain the order in the presentation. But visual aids also prove to be helpful by providing pictures or graphs that many times say much more than words. Videos could also be used if they are brief, well edited, and serve the purpose of the presentation.

Whether or not visual aids are used, the presentation should capture the audience's attention from the beginning, informing them of the purpose of the presentation, motivating the audience to actively listen, and explaining the agenda to be followed. It is also important to say in advance if questions are welcomed during the presentation or if the speaker prefers that they be addressed at the end.

Visual aids must be attractive. Pictures and graphs are better than words, but they must be simple and direct. Every idea should be expressed in only one slide, with a specific title. No single slide should be used to express more than one idea. Unless the presentation requires more time for some reason, it is usually preferable to keep it brief, not using more than 15 to 20 simple slides. In any case, the visual aids must be well ordered and stick to the agenda; the message should be understood from them even if the speaker is not present (some key people may not be able to attend the presentation and they should be able to grasp the essence of the message when receiving it by email).

When making a presentation, the speaker should:

- Maintain eye contact with the audience.

- Speak slowly, clearly, and loudly.

- Avoid any wrong/inappropriate body language.

- Remain within a certain physical area.

ACTIVE LISTENING

Many authors agree that the basic condition for effective interpersonal communication is not to be able to speak or know how to write, despite its importance, but to listen: seek first to understand, then to be understood.

Listening permits us to understand the other person from their own frame of reference, provides very accurate information with which to work, and allows the manager to be better understood and appreciated. Active listening should be directed to the person that is talking, without interfering with their message. Listening involves not only observing what the person is expressing directly, but also trying to understand the meaning behind their words and behavior.

Listening involves using our senses deeply, so that the other perceives that we are interested in what they are saying, and that we are sensitive to their feelings.

Active listening involves:

- Maintaining eye contact.

- Allowing enough time for the meeting.

- Ensuring that we obtain information from the other person sincerely.

- Avoiding touching or offensive acts.

- Repeating the message in your own words in order to verify your understanding.

- Keeping quiet (not interrupting).

- Asking questions to clarify.

- Avoiding distracting gestures.

ORGANIZATIONAL COMMUNICATION

Besides improving their interpersonal communication skills, managers must learn to effectively manage communication within an organization. Good communication is closely related to employees' satisfaction; the lower the uncertainty, the greater the satisfaction. Good communication helps to avoid distortions, ambiguities, and inconsistencies that increase uncertainty and therefore have a negative effect on employee satisfaction. The less distorted communication is, the better employees will understand the management's messages on the goals, policies, and strategies of the company or organization.

Managers should provide the best possible communication (downward, upward, and horizontal) between all levels of the organization:

- Downward communication should have credibility, selectivity, and timing.

- Upward communication is closely linked to downward and should be characterized by freedom of expression so that senior managers do not only hear what they want to hear.

- Horizontal communication, both formal and informal, should be encouraged widely and, like downward and upward communication, must be free from barriers that could restrict it.

Internal communication can be facilitated by encouraging the functioning of an informal social network structure, keeping the company a formal structure that can achieve the stability that is also required. The success and good performance of a company depend on its ability to properly combine the performance of both types of structures.

CORPORATE COMMUNICATION

In large companies, corporate communication, both internal and external, has replaced the old function of "public relations" and refers to how the organization communicates. It includes and integrates aspects of:

- Image
- Identity
- Corporate advertising
- Media relations
- Financial communication
- Employee relations

- Community relations

- Government relations

- Crisis communication

To be effective, corporate communication should be guided by the following principles:

- Clarity

- Honesty

- Opportunity

CHAPTER 6

PROJECT MANAGEMENT

CONCEPT OF PROJECT

In dictionaries, project is defined as a proposal, scheme, or design or as a proposed or planned undertaking. As we see in formal language, the term project is always associated with something that is to be done, something that has not yet taken shape. In technical language, this word has recently begun to be used in the same way. For example, until recently engineers spoke of a project as the design phase of a work, clearly separating it from the construction phase of it. However, today the term project refers to the entire process of conceiving, designing, building, and operating.

It is possible that the increased speed of the modern world, which has forced the design and construction of a work to run concurrently in order to reduce the total execution time, has begun to remove the distinction between phases and consider the project as a whole. Progress in computer systems has facilitated the implementation of many concurrent activities that were previously executed in sequence (for example, the design, procurement, construction, and training of operators in an engineering project).

In many fields, there is also an increase in thinking more in terms of "systems" rather than "parts", thus avoiding the separation between two operations that are so interrelated. In any case, the fact is that when we use the word project today we refer mainly to the entire process of producing a final result. That expression, incidentally, is often used not only in the field of engineering, but in almost all areas of human activity: business, scientific research, advertising, politics, development of war weapons, movies, etc.

In general, we now understand a project to be a set of related temporary activities to elaborate a unique product.

COMMON CHARACTERISTICS OF PROJECTS

The product of a project can be a work of engineering, an information system, a scientific discovery, an advertising campaign, a commercial product, a new war weapon, a movie, etc. Despite such diverse purposes, all projects have certain common characteristics such as:

- They are finite in time (projects have a beginning and an end).

- Their efforts are singular (projects are not repetitive or homogeneous).

- They generate changes in organizations (either through the creation of new systems or facilities or improving existing operations).

- They have their own management requirements (in most cases, projects must be developed through different temporal units and not by the conventional organization).

ORIGINS OF PROJECTS

Projects typically arise in organizations as the result of formal or informal strategic planning processes. They are the final link in a chain that includes:

- The definition of the mission or purpose of the organization.

- The determination of the objectives the organization wants to achieve.

- The formulation of appropriate strategies to achieve those objectives.

- The establishment of programs of action to materialize the strategies.

- The identification of projects in which the established programs are broken.

Besides originating in formal strategic planning processes, projects can also be generated simply as tools to solve a problem or seize an opportunity that is presented to an organization.

CLASSIFICATION OF PROJECTS

The diversity of projects is such that it is difficult to classify them. However, it is possible to classify them according to different criteria:

- Area of work (projects with a focus on engineering, scientific and technological development, business development, economic development, social development, political development, etc.)

- Activity sector (projects undertaken by the public sector and projects undertaken by a company or private organization)

- Purpose (projects aimed at creating a new system, product, or installation and projects aimed at improving something that already exists)

- Product (projects whose product is a service provided during implementation and projects whose product is a commodity or service that can be used later)

- Client (internal projects and projects for external clients)

- Profit (revenue-generating projects and nonprofit projects)

- Development type (projects in which the development of infrastructure predominates and projects in which the generation and use of knowledge predominates)

- Size and complexity (minor or major projects and simple or complex projects)

- Disciplines involved (multidisciplinary projects and projects whose implementation requires the participation of a single discipline of knowledge)

PROJECT MANAGEMENT

Project management is the temporary use of the resources available in an organization to elaborate a unique product.

Project management is a special type of management, different from the functional or permanent management of an organization. The mission of project management is to use certain resources in order to achieve a particular end desired by the organization in a specified period. Although project management uses specific techniques of project planning, scheduling, and control and also uses unconventional organizational structures, its mission or function within the organization should not be confused with the techniques and organizational structures used.

It is generally accepted that project management was born in the military industries in the United States during World War II. This new method emerged due to conventional functional managers' inability to simultaneously run the new major development projects of new weapons or war equipment in addition to their own routines. At the same time, the limitations of the traditional organization to satisfactorily perform projects that required the involvement of various functional departments or divisions were exposed.

It is important to realize that not all projects require project management. Undoubtedly, before World War II, and thus before the birth of the term project management, projects existed and therefore there should have been some form of directing their execution. Until then, projects were generally less complex tasks that could be executed under the direction of conventional managers and performed within the limits of a department or functional division of an organization.

The complexity of projects, coupled with the need for innovation, is the main cause of project management. In principle, an organization or company should create project management units only in the case of complex original efforts of some duration that require resources from different parts of the organization. Acting selectively could save the inevitable conflicts between project managers and managers of permanent units, as well as the inconvenience of constantly changing corporate organization and employees moving between different teams.

Despite the apparent restrictions on the creation of project management units, many corporations have discovered that the difficulties they generate are largely offset in most cases by greater efficiency and effectiveness in operations. This is due to a better focus on the objective, an advantageous concentration of resources, and the precise delegation of authority and responsibility.

Each company or organization must decide, depending on their own situation, whether to use project management on a large or small scale. However, in some sectors, such as engineering consulting, it is the usual way of organizing work.

The functions of project management, as well as those of any other type of management are decision making, organizing, managing staff, planning, controlling, communicating, and directing. However, despite its general identification with ordinary management functions, project management has special characteristics that can be differentiated:

- Its specific activity is related only to a particular project for a limited period, corresponding to the duration of the project.

- It uses resources from various functional units of the organization or company.

- The personnel management function is minimized or limited by the fact that it usually uses people whose selection, training, promotion, and removal corresponds to the functional managers of the organization or company.

- The control function is perhaps the most important, measuring performance, correcting negative deviations, and ensuring compliance with plans.

- The role of direction does not have the same meaning as the functional manager and consists only of a unifying action to achieve project objectives.

- Typically, the project manager defines what should be done in the project and, when it is required, decides with the functional managers how it should be done.

- In general, project management is characterized by its operational nature of temporary duration and focus on the goal of the project. Functional management is strategic, permanent, and related to all the objectives of a corporation.

PROJECT SCOPE

Project scope is the definition of its boundaries and this definition should include the following:

- The problem to solve

- The project's mission

- The project objectives

- The products

- The specifications of products

- The work breakdown structure

Of course, all these elements must be agreed with the client (who hires or receives the outputs of the project) as accurately as possible to avoid inconvenience and ensure project success.

In defining the scope, all restrictions that might influence it, particularly the limitations of time and money, should be taken into account.

Scoping is facilitated by the development of the "work breakdown structure" (WBS). This structure is a hierarchical tree of items or pieces of work that the project team will produce or perform during the project. It represents the identification of the major parts or components that make up the product or final products of the project. Each part or component should be a relatively significant element that can be developed separately for further integration with the rest of the elements.

The usual way to develop the WBS is to subdivide the final product into component parts or "work packages". There are no unique rules to make this division, although the general idea is to identify significant parts that are relatively isolatable from other components. This separation facilitates the implementation of the project, assigning the execution of each component to a particular group and, if possible, to a responsible functional manager.

PROJECT ORGANIZATIONAL STRUCTURE

The organizational structure of a project can be:

- Very simple, consisting only of a project manager and a small collaborating group, with no positions or hierarchies defined.

- Relatively complex, perhaps including managers or assistant managers for each project component and/or for each professional specialty, and a support staff composed of a coordinator, a contract administrator, a planning and control manager, a quality auditor, and a documentation manager, among others, each with their respective collaborators.

In addition, the project manager must choose whether to adopt a rigid or a flexible organization, a centralized or a decentralized organization, and an organization in which all members are working on the project full-time or an organization in which people can participate part-time.

Obviously, relevant organizational decisions depend on the nature, scale, and complexity of the project to be executed. They also depend on the degree of support that the project may receive from the functional departments of the company, which could help to simplify the organization of the project.

EFFICIENT USE OF RESOURCES

The allocation and efficient use of resources must be one of the aspects of greatest concern to the project manager.

Six types of resources for the implementation of a project can be distinguished:

- Money

- People

- Equipment

- Facilities

- Materials

- Information / Technology

In some projects, it is necessary to use the existing available resources. In others, it is possible to select the required resources to a greater or lesser degree. In any case, the duration and cost of the project will be related to the resources available.

If many resources are available and they are very efficient, it could be possible to reduce the duration of the project, but it may be more costly. Consequently, care should be taken in each project to achieve the best possible balance between resources, duration, and cost, depending on the project objectives.

Resources should be specified according to the project schedule. The allocation of resources should be controlled in order to avoid too many fluctuations in the quantity and type of resources throughout the project. In general, it is neither feasible nor desirable that resources are used for a very short time and reused later for an equally short time. It is preferable, in general, to keep them for longer periods of time, but not to allow them to become idle.

PROJECT HUMAN RESOURCES

The most important resources for project implementation are people, or human resources. People who are integrated into the project team should be chosen based on their knowledge, skills, and ability to effectively collaborate with others.

A common problem in the formation of project teams is that it is often difficult to count on the most qualified people for each role, as they may be busy working on other projects or on other tasks for the organization to which they belong. However, it is necessary to make every effort to get suitable people who preferably know each other and have worked together successfully on previous projects, since trust between team members greatly facilitates the integration of the project team.

Companies or organizations that manage many projects simultaneously must establish some kind of procedure for the best possible allocation of human resources to different projects, taking into account the characteristics of each project and its importance to the overall strategy of the company or organization. In general, this process involves organizing the projects into programs or sets of related projects that share the same type of resources, therefore managing the project portfolio of the company in order to carry out projects with less risk and more favorable impact on the company or organization.

The distribution of responsibilities is the assignment of rights and duties of the various managers and supervisors involved in the project, both from the project organization and for the client organization, clearly indicating the levels of authority and decision of each of them.

In order to avoid confusion, especially in complex projects, a responsibility matrix must be developed. A responsibility matrix is a table that lists the persons or units responsible for carrying out each piece of work in the WBS. It defines who has the primary responsibility of each component of the work, who is responsible for support, who should report to whom, and who has authority to approve every major action.

PROJECT COST ESTIMATION

Having defined the necessary resources in the project as well as its magnitude and distribution over time, the costs for these resources should be estimated. The estimated cost of the project should be reviewed and adjusted as the project develops. Of course, the margin of error in this estimate will diminish as more precise information on the resources and their cost becomes available.

There are different techniques of cost estimation, whose use in a given project will depend on the scope and nature of the project and the project phase or stage in which the estimate is made. Among the cost estimation techniques are:

- Estimation by analogy, using the cost data of similar projects already implemented as the basis for estimating project costs.

- Parameter estimation, using project characteristics (parameters) to estimate the cost of a project based on the parametric cost information available from other projects.

- Aggregated estimate, estimating the cost of individual items and adding them until total project costs are estimated.

The application of cost estimation techniques can be facilitated by the use of mathematical models and computer tools if the complexity of the project requires it.

PROJECT BUDGET

The budget is the financial expression of a project plan. Project budget is the relation of the expenses that are necessary to implement the project, determining the time of occurrence and discriminating by concepts or components of expenditure (materials, equipment, labor, overhead, supervision, etc.); however, other types of budgets may be required according to the nature of the project: income budget, cash budget, etc.

Usually, the spending budget is accompanied by cost estimates that serve as its support, indicating their associated degree of certainty, which depend on the nature of the project and the level of detail in its definition. It is also usual to present a "cost breakdown structure" (CBS) in correspondence with the WBS.

PROJECT SCHEDULE

Project schedule is a timetable that shows how the required activities are sequenced and phased over the allotted period.

An activity is a time-consuming task to be performed in the project. The activities in which the project is subdivided are based on the project scope, preferably from the WBS. Activities should be defined as the process steps for obtaining each of the products of the project.

The list of activities for each product must be as complete and detailed as possible. Then they can be grouped to the extent that it is appropriate to do so, taking into account factors such as the responsibility for their implementation and the time required. Grouping activities is always possible if two conditions are met. The first is that the same person responsible for executing all tasks in a group, so as not to create confusion regarding the responsibility for implementation. The second is that the collective execution time is not excessive, which would make it difficult to control the progress as discussed below.

Once activities are defined, the next step is to specify which activities must precede others and which are to be executed concurrently. The time required to perform each activity should also be estimated. The estimated duration of each activity is usually made based on the experience of previous projects.

To avoid unpleasant surprises, the estimated duration of each activity must be calculated carefully, taking into account any element that could affect it. No activity should take too much time, which would make it difficult to verify whether a possible delay in its execution will affect the entire project and would not allow timely corrections. In general, no activity that requires more than four to six weeks (preferably no more than two weeks) to execute should be specified. Activities that do not last long enough, for example less than a day, should also not be established.

Since the project is divided into phases and activities, some sort of schedule or timetable is required to express the sequence, timing of implementation, and interrelationship of each of them. This allows measuring compliance and implementing the necessary adjustments. The schedule is a diagram showing the location and length in time of the various activities required to implement the project. The schedule should indicate the milestones or checkpoints that will allow to assess project progress and to verify compliance with the plan. This tool is usually a chart or graph, distinguishing between bar charts and network diagrams.

A. Bar chart

The best known bar chart for project control is the "Gantt chart" designed by the American engineer Henry L. Gantt in the early twentieth century. This chart simply consists of a coordinate system shown:

- On the horizontal axis, a schedule or timeline, defined in terms of the most appropriate unit to the work to be executed (hour, day, week, month, etc.).

- On the vertical axis, the activities that constitute the work to be executed.

Each activity is mapped with a horizontal line or bar whose length is proportional to its duration and whose measurement is made with respect to the scale set on the horizontal axis.

Further information on the required resources can be placed in the Gantt chart, indicating the time when they are needed, corresponding to the period of implementation of activities that require it. For this purpose, additional graphics could also be used, such as a graph in which the horizontal axis remains as a record of the time scale and on the vertical axis the resources are listed, representing the period of their use with horizontal lines or bars.

The main advantage of the Gantt chart is that its use requires a minimum level of planning. Gantt charts are very effective in simple projects or for a simplified view of the control of complex projects. However, it does not show the relationship between activities, does not offer conditions for the analysis of options, and does not take into account factors such as cost, so its use is quite limited in sizable projects.

B. Network diagrams

Network diagrams emerged in the late 1950s as an alternative to bar charts for controlling complex projects. Network diagrams show the relationships among various project activities. One of the most popular methods is the "critical path method" (CPM) developed by the DuPont company. The other is the "technical assessment and review program" or "program evaluation and review technique" (PERT), developed by the U.S. Navy and the consulting group Booz, Allen, and Hamilton. Overall, the initial difference between the two methods was due to the use of probabilities in the PERT method for estimating the timing of activities, focusing on this element, while the CPM method focused on the cost estimates and were deterministic. Currently however, the two systems are integrated, so that it is common to designate the joint acronym PERT/CPM as one system.

The basic concepts used in network diagrams are events and activities. An event is the initiation or completion of a task, but not its implementation. The actual execution of a task or job is an activity. An event is associated with a date while an activity is associated with time. Events are usually represented by circles and activities are identified with arrows. Each arrow or activity joins two circles or events in the diagram.

Once the activities are defined, including their duration and their relationship, the diagram is drawn, respecting the sequence established between activities. In order to avoid confusion, it is not right that two events are directly linked by more than one activity. To avoid this, ghosts or link activities with no duration, are created. Events are then numbered and the earliest start date, the latest start date, the earliest completion date, and the latest date of completion of each activity, according to the estimates of duration of the activity and the duration of activities preceding it, are determined.

The critical path in a network diagram is the most time-consuming activities path. It therefore determines the shortest possible time of project implementation. Activities that are not on the critical path have some slack for execution as long as it does not affect the total project duration. By contrast, activities on the critical path have no slack and if delayed, it will cause a delay in project completion.

PROJECT MANAGEMENT SOFTWARE

Since the use of computers became widespread, project management software based on the PERT/CPM technique has been developed which facilitates control of project time and cost, providing the project manager progress reports that allow him not only know the degree of compliance with the established schedule and budget forecasts, but to have options to analyze and make the necessary adjustments and resolve resource allocation problems.

Some of this software, with relative advantages and disadvantages of cost and ease of use are:

- Artemis Project Management Software

- Deltek Open Plan

- Intuit QuickBase Project Management

- Microsoft Project

- Open Workbench

- Oracle Primavera Project Management Professional

- SAP Project Management

It is essential to remember that the usefulness of these programs depends on the accuracy and timeliness of the basic information, the maintenance of adequate collection systems, and the processing of such information.

These programs or commercial packages could be used alone or integrated in platforms which connect to other systems of the organization or company, taking advantage of internet technology. The latter is more frequent in large organizations that manage many projects.

PROJECT RISK MANAGEMENT

Risk is the exposure of the project to contingencies affecting the achievement of project objectives.

Reducing the likelihood that the project may fail to meet its requirements of time, cost, and quality is the objective of risk analysis, and it should be part of project planning.

Risk management seeks to identify, assess, and respond to project risks in order to minimize the likelihood and the consequences of adverse events on the achievement of the project goal. Risk management must occur repeatedly throughout the project.

A. Identification of the risk

Risk identification involves determining which risks may adversely affect the project's objective and what might be the consequences of each of them if they occur. Risk identification involves answering the following questions: What could go wrong? What could prevent the project from achieving its objectives?

The many factors that may pose risks in a project can be grouped into several categories:

- Factors derived from resource constraints, such as time and money

- Factors derived from natural causes or force majeure: theft, fire, strikes, terrorism, etc.

- Factors derived from legal changes or changes in financing conditions

- Factors arising from technological changes or inadequate use of technologies

- Factors arising from inaccuracies in the project, the behavior of people and project management

B. Risk assessment

Assessment of each risk involves determining the probability that the risk event will occur and the degree of impact the event will have on the project objective. One can distinguish between qualitative and quantitative risk analysis.

Qualitative risk analysis involves estimating the likelihood of the occurrence of identified risks and determining its potential consequences for the project. There are different techniques to perform this analysis, but most of them are based on determining the probability of failure of the identified risk factors and the consequences of such failures.

Quantitative analysis involves estimating the cost or economic impact a risk would have on the project if it did occur.

The combination of qualitative and quantitative risk analysis allows the estimation of the risk of the project, according to the following equation:

$$\text{Risk (R)} = \text{Probability of failure (P)} \times \text{Impact (I)}$$

According to the level of assessed risk, risks can be classified as high, moderate, or low.

C. Risk Response

The planning response to risk is the development of an action plan to reduce the impact or likelihood of each risk.

The development of risk responses implies that measures or actions that reduce the potential for damage for all risk factors must be devised, with emphasis on those factors that are considered critical. As many of these actions cost money, there must be an appropriate balance between the cost of such measures and the total project costs and an appropriate allocation of such costs among the various factors, according to the respective level of risk.

The measures usually recommended to reduce the risks in project implementation include:

- Using external consultants to review the design.

- Incorporating quality requirements in the equipment specifications.

- Performing a suppliers capacity analysis in the selection of procurement sources.

- Using quality auditing techniques.

- Developing periodic progress reports to verify the status of the project.

Of course, in addition to specific measures that reduce risks, the following is necessary:

- Proper selection of the project manager and the people who integrate into the project team

- The use of work processes whose quality is certified

- Good understanding between the client and project manager, with respect to product specifications and any other relevant aspect of the project

The risk response plan should not be limited to identifying risks and recommending measures to reduce them. There is also the need to develop contingency plans. A contingency plan is a predefined set of actions to be implemented if the risk event occurs. It responds to the following question: If it happens, what are we going to do?.

D. Risk monitoring and control

Monitoring and controlling risks implies applying the risk management plan in order to respond to risk events over the course of the project.

PROJECT COMMUNICATIONS MANAGEMENT

Communication in a project is the exchange of information within and outside the project organization. Communications planning involves determining the information and communication needs of all stakeholders in the project and defining how to meet those needs.

A. Effective Communication

To communicate effectively, people must have the desire to communicate, understand the communication process, communicate clearly and honestly, and verify the proper response in their attempts to communicate.

B. Communication Levels

In a project, it is often important to distinguish two levels of communication:

- Internal communication (within the project team)

- External communication (with the organization's senior management, clients, and other external project stakeholders)

All important information concerning the project should be communicated with transparency and consistency to all who need it. There should be as much communication within the project as possible, although precise rules for communication outside of the project must be established, especially for formal aspects or facts that can generate unwanted conflict in the relationship with the client.

In addition to formal communication, it is very important to encourage informal communication within the project team. Good relationships between people often depend on the formation of interpersonal communication networks independent of formal communication. The more contact and exchange of information between the members of the project team, the more likely they will be to have the information needed to do their job better and they will be better able to cooperate and collaborate with others. Informal communication is also desirable between the project team and the client, but in this case, as already noted, the critical issues related to a communication project must correspond only to the project manager or any other person authorized by him to do so in order to avoid any unnecessary and unpleasant conflicts.

C. Communications Plan

The communications plan is a document that defines how communications will be managed in the project. It must state the type of information required by each project stakeholder and the means and frequency with which that information must be provided.

The communications plan should include:

- The methodology to be used to collect and store various types of information.

- The structure of information distribution (written reports, meetings, e- mails, mail, intranet, fax, video conferencing, internet, database access, etc.).

- A description of information (format, content, level of detail, definitions, and conventions to be used).

- An information production schedule (when to produce and deliver each piece of information).

- Methods of access to information.

- A procedure to update the communication plan.

D. Information Required

Information is the result of collecting, processing, and analyzing data related to a project in order to increase the level of knowledge about it. In this sense, it is necessary to distinguish between the basic information needed to implement the project and the information necessary to control its execution. Both types of information must be reliable, complete, and timely in order for the project to be carried out satisfactorily.

The information needed to control the execution depends on the nature of the project and the management levels established in the organizational structure of the project. Lower level managers, if the complexity of the project makes them necessary, require detailed information of operations that they are in charge of. However, for senior managers, it is enough to receive summarized information on the state of the project and reports of any deviation from project expectations.

Management information must be accurate, timely, complete, and concise. Furthermore, its cost must be proportional to the utility it provides to the managers.

In very simple projects, manual management information systems may suffice, but the availability of specialized computer programs at a relatively low cost makes it very convenient and almost essential to use them in order to provide necessary management information on most projects.

Companies must possess the ability to retain and analyze data and historical information from their projects in order to use them in future projects.

E. Management Information Systems

In most projects, it is necessary to provide specific information systems, since corporate information systems can be inadequate or even non-existent. A management information system is a group of methods and procedures aimed at managers which distribute information needed for planning, organizing, directing, and controlling the activities of the project.

The usual components or subsystems of a management information system for project control are:

- Schedule

- Resource Allocation

- Budget

- Timesheets

- Progress Reports

- Procurement

- Accounting and Billing

- Control Reports

- Results Forecast

A management information system project should be able to generate reports or progress reports that are required by various stakeholders in the project according to their needs. Progress reports are usually related to the control of the project, so they are usually comprised of results of the time, cost, and quality control of the project and recommendations to overcome any observed failures and prevent future problems.

PROJECT PRESENTATION FOR APPROVAL

Projects need to be formulated in clear and precise terms to facilitate their evaluations, which are done by those who will authorize their execution and the financial institutions which are expected to facilitate loans to carry them out.

There are no uniform rules for the formulation of projects, although some companies or financial entities often establish guidelines or instructions to do so.

Overall, the presentation of a draft for approval must answer the following questions:

- *What is to be done?* The answer to this question is a description of the scope of the project, its nature, and the products or outcomes expected from it.

- *Why do we do it?* The answer to this question involves an explanation of the rationale for the project, the reasons for its implementation, the benefits to be derived, and the consequences that would exist if the project were to fail.

- *How will it be done?* The answer to this question is a description of the methodology and work plan for the execution of the project, including an explanation of the required activities and how to carry them out, the needs of procurement of equipment and materials, and the applicable laws.

- *Who will do it?* The answer to this question is a description of the organization established for the project and the main companies and individuals who participate in it, defining the responsibilities of each relevant participant. Identification of the project manager and the reasons for their choice is a fundamental aspect of an organization.

- *When is it going to happen?* The answer to this question is a description of the start and end dates of the project and an overview of the implementation schedule.

- *How much will it cost?* The answer to this question involves an estimate of project costs, including the investment needed to develop the project and the operating expenses. Project investments are a creation of capital, increasing the productive capacity of the implementing company. Investments should be differentiated depending on the type of currency (domestic or foreign) and broken down into various components. The estimated investment costs should indicate the margin of error and estimation methods employed. Operating costs and expenses are those which will be incurred after any initial investments are made and the project operation is initiated.

- *How will it be paid?* The answer to this question involves information on sources of funds for project execution, whether they are resources from the executing company, contributions from the project partners, income from the advance sale of products, or loans from financial institutions.

- *What guarantees the success of the project?* The answer to this question involves an identification of the main risks of the project, measures that will be taken to prevent or reduce these risks, and the results of any previous study that has been conducted to determine the feasibility of the project.

The document presenting the project for approval is often called a "project charter", and once approved, becomes a mandate of action for the project team.

PROJECT EVALUATION

After the project has been formulated, including a definition of its financial aspects, its evaluation can proceed. The evaluation, which aims to analyze the feasibility and desirability of the project, can be performed by the organization itself or by external entities, usually those that are expected to contribute to its funding.

Depending on the nature and scope of the project, evaluation can be a fairly complex task. A full assessment of a project may include the following types of analysis:

- Technical evaluation

- Economic evaluation

- Financial evaluation

- Social assessment

- Institutional assessment

- Environmental assessment

In addition to the above types of assessment, some financial institutions, particularly multilateral government agencies, require stakeholder analysis and gender analysis. The stakeholder analysis is done to identify the stakeholders in the project or those that may have some influence on it, in order to determine their degree of resistance or acceptance of the project. Gender analysis is usually done to ensure that women are not excluded from project benefits.

A. Technical evaluation

A technical evaluation is done to analyze the technical feasibility of the project and includes a review of basic data (size, location, period of performance, technology), as well as the cost estimates presented. This review should determine whether all relevant technical factors have been taken into account, the alternatives have been properly compared, the available resources are being used appropriately, and project costs have been estimated correctly.

B. Economic evaluation

An economic evaluation is done to compare economic benefits to the economic costs required to implement the project in order to determine if it is worth the investment.

To perform an economic evaluation, all benefits and economic costs of the project must be estimated and expressed in the same basis. In some cases, this estimate is a fairly simple process. In others, the intervention of economists may be required to include an adequate analysis of the distortions in the economy, opportunity costs, and effects on the balance of payments, transfer payments, and other similar concepts. This analysis has been called "social evaluation". In any case, an economic evaluation is usually based on estimating the profitability of the project by calculating the net present value, internal rate of return, or benefit-cost ratio.

Because of the uncertainty present in most estimates of economic benefits and costs of a project, an economic evaluation generally includes a sensitivity and risk analysis, taking into account possible variations in the values of the basic elements.

C. Financial evaluation

The financial evaluation is done to determine whether or not the necessary funds will be available to carry out the project and whether it will be able to generate enough revenue to recover the costs incurred. A financial analysis includes the consideration of the financial profitability of a project and its impact on the financial situation of the corporation that will undertake it, as well as a review of financial projections, expected financial statements, sources and uses of funds, estimates of revenue and expenditure, and a payback plan.

D. Social assessment

The social assessment is done to review the validity of project assumptions about its external social conditions, determine the degree of cultural acceptance of the project, and analyze its social impact. By social evaluation, economic evaluation of the project is also understood, considering relevant costs and benefits for the economy as a whole and not only those relevant to the executing organization. However, it seems more appropriate to consider this as a form of economic evaluation and reserve the term "social assessment" for social analysis itself.

E. Institutional Assessment

An institutional assessment is done to determine the legal competence and the experience of the implementing organization in relation to the proposed project, including a review of its management capacity, internal controls, and coordination problems with other institutions. In some cases, strengthening of the institutional capacity of the implementing organization or providing institutional coordination mechanisms before carrying out a complex project are required. Prior training of the project's technical, administrative, and managerial staff may also be required.

F. Environmental Assessment

An environmental assessment is done to identify, interpret, and prevent the consequences or effects that a project may cause to health and human welfare and ecosystems in which man lives and on which he depends. In many countries the presentation of an environmental impact study is required for any development project, which should include a project description and actions, a description of the environment, a description of viable alternatives, identification of potential impacts of proposed action, a definition of preventive and/or mitigating potential impacts of planned measures, and an implementation schedule of environmental protection measures. The World Bank and many other international financial institutions also require the submission of environmental impact studies as a requirement for evaluation in projects that they are to finance.

PROJECT MANAGER

The project manager is the person appointed by the performing organization to achieve the project objectives. The project manager is usually the key figure in project implementation. The project manager is responsible for all aspects of the project. They do not directly perform all activities, but they are responsible for properly carrying them out. When the project manager abdicates their conductive responsibility, disaster strikes.

A. Responsibility of the project manager

The primary responsibility of the project manager is to carry out the project within the requirements of time, cost, and quality. In addition to this overall responsibility, the project manager must:

- Define what to do in the project to achieve its goals.

- Decide when to perform each activity.

- Explain why each activity is needed.

- Determine the necessary funds to implement the project.

- Ensure the timely allocation of resources in the project.

- Integrate the various activities and promote full and timely communication between people in the project.

- Evaluate how well the project is progressing.

- Resolve conflicts.

- Represent the project to the client and to the authorities of the corporation.

- Communicate results.

A project manager, as well as any professional, also has a responsibility to their profession and to society. In particular, they should:

- Uphold ethical values and respect for the laws, rules, and regulations applicable to their work.

- Continuously improve their knowledge, skills, and abilities.

- Seek the common good and the satisfaction of all stakeholders in every project that they manage.

- Share best practices and lessons learned in the course of his business with their team members and other project managers.

B. Competencies of the project manager

Like any manager, a project manager should possess:

- Managerial and conceptual skills or the ability to see the organization as a whole and understand the significance of the project.

- People skills or the ability to effectively manage a group of people.

- Technical skills or knowledge of technologies related to the project.

A project manager must be given sufficient authority to make decisions, set policies relating to the project, organize the team, manage project funds, monitor deadlines and implementation costs, select and oversee contractors or subcontractors, and manage the external relations of the project.

Obviously, it is not enough to be officially granted that authority. A project manager with experience and prestige should be able to exercise it, especially in regard to members of his staff, since they normally do not have formal line authority over them. He does not need to be the greatest expert in the subject of the project, but he must understand the work being done, so as to win the confidence of the team, particularly in the case of teams that are known for their technical skill.

The project manager must be a leader of leaders. He cannot act alone. He should make all members of the project organization feel that they are leaders too. He should choose competent collaborators and give them leeway. Like every leader, he should lead by example.

C. Task of the project manager

The task of the project manager is to articulate the values of the project's organization, creating a system in which people can be productive and explain the goals that the system must achieve. They must respect people and leverage existing cultural values. Additionally, they must ensure the effective support of the senior management of the organization and serve as a liaison between corporate management, the project team, and the client.

The project manager must prevent crisis situations so that they do not occur, but if they happen he must act decisively and firmly, without pretense or hesitation. Most projects are very demanding process, with a lot of stress and frequent conflicts between different objectives. Therefore, a project manager must have sufficient strength of character and strength of will to face difficult situations.

The project manager has the difficult task of balancing:

- The implementation of the project with the dynamics of the environment.

- Project needs with the needs of the team members.

- The cost, duration, and quality of the project.

- The total system and the various subsystems of the project.

D. Selecting the project manager

Proper selection of a project manager is perhaps the most important decision a company must make to ensure the desired results in a project. One will never find the perfect manager who possesses all the necessary conditions of knowledge, experience, integrity, passion, vision, authenticity, conviction, persistence, etc., so it will always be necessary to choose the best possible candidate in accordance with the requirements of each project, giving them the proper support so they can accomplish the project goals.

Project management is currently a professional specialty, so people designated as project managers should have adequate experience in this activity. Technical knowledge related to the project is convenient and even necessary, but it is not sufficient to qualify a person as project manager. In addition to the knowledge and personal qualities that we have identified, a project manager should be shaped by the study of the principles and techniques of project management, participation as a collaborator in projects under the guidance of experienced managers, and the assumption of progressive management responsibilities in increasingly complex and significant projects. This learning process can be shorter or longer depending on the conditions of the individual and the opportunities given to him, but it must be met in order to take responsibility for leading a major project.

E.   Managing the project team

A key element in a project's success is the human factor. The progress of a project will depend on the project manager understanding this fact, recognizing the value of the informal organization, having sincere concern and respect for his team, and behaving ethically. The project manager should be a dynamic element of the project, giving inspiration and creating a powerful force around himself.

A successful project manager shows confidence in the integrity, ability, and motivation of team members. He focuses on the human aspects of the problems of the people that he leads, setting only general performance goals instead of trying to keep people actively engaged in carrying out a series of specified work in a prescribed manner. An effective project manager also has a commitment to the training and development of people working on the project.

CONFLICT MANAGEMENT IN PROJECTS

Implementing a project almost always generates challenges that go beyond the provisions of the planning stage. The difficulties are greater when the project represents a major innovation or change from previous projects or situations.

There is abundant humorous literature on the problems of project implementation. The following are referred to "the laws of project management":

- "No project finishes on time, within budget, and with the same starting staff. Yours will not be the first."

- "Projects progress quickly until achieving 90% of completion, then they stay at 90% forever."

- "An advantage of the confusing objectives of the project is that it releases you from the cumbersome task of estimating the corresponding costs."

- "When things are going well, something bad will happen. When they cannot get worse, they will. When things seem to go better, you've forgotten to consider something."

- "If the scope of the project is allowed to change freely, the rate of change will exceed the rate of progress."

- "No system is free of traps. Attempts to remove the traps inevitably introduce new traps."

- "Project teams detest progress reports that highlight the lack of progress."

- "A carelessly planned project takes three times as long to complete as expected. One that is carefully planned will take twice as long."

Although they seem exaggerated, these "laws of project management" reveal many real situations that a project manager needs to prevent and control. Among the difficulties that often emerge when trying to implement a project are the following:

- The execution takes longer than expected.

- Major problems that were previously unidentified arise.

- Coordination of activities is not sufficiently effective.

- Other projects and business problems distract attention from the project.

- The capabilities of the people involved are not sufficiently adequate.

- The training of lower level people is inadequate.

- Uncontrollable factors have adverse impacts.

In the project environment, conflicts are inevitable. These difficulties can generate various types of conflicts:

- Conflicts on deadlines
- Conflicts on project scope
- Conflicts on project priorities
- Conflicts on people assigned
- Conflicts on technical matters
- Conflicts on administrative procedures
- Personality conflicts
- Conflicts on costs

To prevent difficulties and conflicts in a project, the project manager should take measures to facilitate effective implementation of the project. These preventive measures are:

- Proper communication between all participants.
- Appropriate conceptualization of the project.
- Commitment and involvement of people.
- Provision of adequate resources.
- Development of an implementation plan.

Additionally, the project manager must ensure that:

- The scope, time, and expected cost to implement the project are consistent with the requirements and the ability of the people involved.
- Project planning considers all relevant aspects and includes an adequate analysis of the risks in the execution.
- Adequate coordination exists between project members and the rest of the company.

- The skills and training of staff are adequate enough to successfully execute the project.

- The relationship with the client is as efficient and transparent as possible and his expectations are clearly defined.

- The methods, techniques and procedures to be used in the project are adequate and its suitability and quality are properly verified.

When handling a conflict with the intention of resolving it, the first thing to do is separate problems from people. When problems can be judged objectively, without emotional or personal interest factors involved, it may be relatively easy to find a solution. When people are part of the problem, the project manager needs to talk with them separately, using a mediator if appropriate, until reaching a solution. If this does not work, it might be necessary to relocate the troublemakers or remove them from the project.

SUCCESSFUL PROJECTS

A successful project is one that not only complies with all cost, time, and quality requirements, but does so to the satisfaction of all stakeholders in the project: client, users, project team, suppliers, financiers, government regulators, unions, managers of the company executing the project, etc. Meeting all these requirements and expectations is a difficult task that the project manager faces when implementing a project.

The features that are consistently present in successful projects in all sectors include:

- Agreement between the project team, client, and company management regarding project goals.

- A plan showing an overall path and clear responsibilities that can be used to measure progress during the project implementation.

- Consistent and effective communication between everyone involved in the project.

- A controlled scope.

- Support from the management of the company.

- Other general recommendations for the success of a project are to:

- Allocate adequate resources.

- Delegate authority to the project manager.

- Maintain a positive organizational climate.

- Maintain updated documentation in accordance with the methodology of work.

- Control the execution.

- Ensure the adoption of changes and partial results.

- Perform an orderly shutdown.

- Check client satisfaction.

In projects of economic or social development in the public sector, it will also be necessary to ensure broad social support for the project and ensure that it will be able to overcome the restrictions of the institutional context, financial problems, political changes of officials, and priorities that often hamper this type of project.

The possibilities of implementing a project within the time and cost normally desired increase if its conceptual phase and its definition phase are performed correctly, anticipating risks and taking appropriate preventative actions.

MANAGEMENT OF CHANGES

Even if a project has been well planned, it is likely that contingencies arise during implementation, forcing the project manager to make changes in the plans. If these changes are handled properly and they are approved by the client, they should not constitute conflict factors. Therefore, good communication between the project manager and the client is essential to ensure project success.

In general, changes with impact on the price of the contract may be due to:

- Changes in scope due to changes in client or project needs.

- Increased cost of resources used in project implementation.

- Changes in regulations or standards affecting project implementation.

- The need for a contractor to carry out activities that are not foreseen in the contract or are supposed to be performed or provided by the customer.

- Extension of the duration of the project for reasons not attributable to the contractor.

For the proper management of changes, so that they do not become an unnecessary source of conflict, it is necessary to establish a suitable system for processing changes from the beginning. It is usual, especially in larger projects, to have a contract administrator within the project organization. One of their main functions is to prepare a request for necessary changes and submit it to the client, after being given permission by the project manager.

Change management should usually follow the following procedure:

- Identification of the problem (the need for change)

- Evaluation of alternative solutions

- Selection of the best alternative or option

- Preparation of the change or claim

- Negotiation with the client

- Implementation of the agreement

During the execution of a project, the customer relationship should be governed by a contract. However, the contract is often forgotten and conditions not specified in the contract are often accepted, which is a source of difficulty and possible economic loss and can disrupt client relationship and hinder fair claims processing. All necessary changes with respect to the initial conditions of the contract must be formally approved by the persons competent to do so before its execution, in order to avoid any inconvenience.

CHAPTER 7

STRATEGIC PLANNING AND IMPLEMENTATION

STRATEGIC MANAGEMENT

Strategic management is the process of formulating, implementing, and evaluating the strategy of a company. Strategic management is not to be confused with strategic planning, as the latter is a part of strategic management and refers only to strategy formulation.

Strategic management is complemented by and related to operational management, but differs from it in that strategic management is more focused on the medium and long-term company needs whereas operational management is more focused on short-term needs.

Early attempts to define approaches or schools of strategic management began in the 1950s and have been formalized since the 1970s. The main approaches or schools of strategic management are:

- The school of strategic planning. This school sees the creation of strategy as a formal process in which strategies are determined by the internal strengths and weaknesses and external opportunities and threats.

- School of positioning. This school conceives strategy formation as an analytical process of evaluating the competitive position of the company in the sector to which it belongs.

- School of entrepreneurship. This school sees the creation of strategy as an intuitive process based on the vision of the entrepreneur.

- School of learning. This school conceives strategy making as a learning process based on experience.

- Environmental school. This school conceives strategy formation as an adjustment to the conditions imposed by the external environment.

- School of vision based on resource. This school conceives strategy creation as the development and flexible and efficient use of resources and capabilities of the firm (knowledge, leadership, skills, competencies, etc.).

Although the predominance of one approach over another has varied over time, almost all of them are used more or less frequently, often in combination. However, it can be said that the prevailing approach today, at least in the academic sphere, is the resource-based view. This approach seeks to analyze the actual options that are presented to the company and use the resources (leadership, knowledge, core competencies, experience, learning, culture, human resources, etc.) as quickly as possible to take advantage of these options, developing new skills and competencies and continuously maintaining a constant rate of innovation.

CORPORATE GOVERNANCE, ETHICS AND SOCIAL RESPONSIBILITY

Strategy can be formulated in any business context, but the ideal is that the company possesses good corporate governance and acts with ethics and social responsibility.

The concept of corporate governance refers to the set of principles and rules that guide the design, integration, and operation of the governing bodies of the company: shareholders, the board, and the executive directors. Good corporate governance provides incentives to protect the interests of the company and the shareholders, ensure the creation of value, make efficient use of resources, and provide transparency of information.

Ethics is a set of moral standards used to judge whether something is right or wrong. Companies and people choose between good and evil based on their own moral code. Managers can influence the ethics of a company condemning the lack of ethics and educating employees to apply the three-question test (Is it lawful? Is it fair? How does it make me feel?) when faced with ethical dilemmas. Unfortunately, many managers give bad examples and act unethically by misleading their customers and shareholders, extorting suppliers, disrespecting employees, and not complying with the legal obligations of the company.

We need to measure success in terms of the results obtained not only for the company, but for others. What is really needed in business is to leave a mark in time, helping to make the good things in life available and accessible to more people.

Social responsibility is the concern that companies have for the welfare of society. It implies obligations that go beyond profit or compliance with the law. Today, corporate philanthropy is moving from help for the needy to strategic grants, which are more closely related to the mission or goals of the company, and they direct donations to the places where they operate.

MISSION, VISION, AND VALUES

Before starting the strategic planning process, or as the first step in the process, the definition of the mission and vision of the company should be made clear.

A. Mission

The mission statement of the company is an explanation of its reason for being. Essentially, it is the answer to the question: What is our business?

The mission statement clarifies the nature and purpose of the company and resolves divergent opinions. The essential elements of the mission include a clear definition of company customers, products, and services; the markets in which it operates; and the values and practices by which it wishes to be recognized.

An analysis of the missions of various companies reveals that not all companies seem to state their mission clearly and directly, although almost all express the market sectors to which its activity is oriented in a fairly general way. Mission statements often include expressions that are aspirations of the company, such as "to be leaders in the market", "satisfy our customers" ,"provide an excellent service", "be profitable", "act with integrity", "offer new, high-quality products", "be the preferred supplier to our customers", "contribute to the development of the country", etc. Among the most original mission statements, which deviate slightly from the above mentioned pattern, is the 3M mission: "Solve problems innovatively".

B. Vision

In addition to the mission statement, almost all companies develop a vision statement of the company. This statement is an answer to the question: What do we want to be?

A vision statement is important to determine the long-term objectives of a company and align the entire organization in that direction. The vision statement usually includes the establishment of the position that the company wants to achieve and defines the contribution it intends to make to society.

As in the mission, the vision statement is usually an expression of aspirations of the company, so it is often confused with the mission. Indeed, some companies have identical mission and vision statements. The vision statements of most companies often include words such as "be recognized for (innovation, quality, social responsibility, profitability, etc.)", "satisfy our customers", "provide complete and integrated solutions to our customers", "create value for our shareholders and customers", "act effectively", "respect", "lead", "act with integrity", "be the preferred supplier of our customers" , etc.

The importance of mission and vision statements does not lie only in the creation of a favorable image of the company. If employees do not have a clear idea of the business and objectives of the company, they will operate in an erroneous context and the desired results will not be achieved.

C. Values

Some companies, in addition to their mission and vision statements, explicitly set the values or principles that they want to govern their actions. Market orientation and customer satisfaction appear as the most frequent values. Other values usually mentioned are quality, respect, innovation, excellence, and teamwork.

Although one cannot generalize, the impression left by the values statements of many companies is that they collect a number of concepts that sound good, but are not necessarily accompanied by the will to practice them or the concrete actions to ensure compliance in the company.

STRATEGIC PLANNING

Many companies set their goals, objectives, and strategies through orderly processes of strategic planning. Strategic planning includes defining steps to move from the current situation of the company to a desired situation or target.

A. Stages of strategic planning

The steps of the strategic planning processes are usually:

- External analysis

- Internal analysis

- Balance of internal and external analysis

- Definition of strategic objectives

- Selection of corporate strategies

It is important to recognize that strategic planning is a dynamic process that does not end. Companies must be constantly evaluating their strategies and formulating new strategic plans.

B. Principles of strategic planning

The following have been proposed as principles of strategic planning:

- Feasibility (that which is planned should be feasible)

- Objectivity and quantification (plans should be based on real data and precise and accurate reasoning)

- Flexibility (plans should allow margins of slack to face unforeseen situations)

- Unity (all specific business plans should be integrated into an overall plan)

- Dynamism (when a plan is implemented, it may become necessary to reformulate it completely)

C. Errors in strategic planning

Some common errors in strategic planning processes include:

- Not including the participation of employees and other stakeholders of the company in the process: shareholders, customers, partners, and suppliers. Some companies delegate strategic planning in a planning group, sometimes formed by external consultants, unaware that a plan is better and easier to implement when the stakeholders of the company have been involved in its formulation.

- Making it a routine and uncreative process. Sometimes companies transform their strategic planning processes into tedious, time consuming procedures that end up being more "tactical" than "strategic".

- Guiding it towards producing overly rigid and detailed plans. Traditional strategic planning documents have been developed to become a rule of action for each business activity, regardless of the uncertainty of the environment that may make it necessary to modify them to prevent failure.

- Not communicating the plan to employees. It makes no sense to keep the strategic plan secret, without communicating it to the employees that must have participated in its elaboration and whose cooperation is essential to the achievement of the objectives of the company. However, it is a frequent practice in many companies with an exaggerated sense of confidentiality.

- Assuming that a small or medium business does not require strategic planning. Although it is likely that a small or medium company is limited in its possibilities of action, due to the lack of adequate resources, it still needs a strategic planning process tailored to its abilities and needs.

EXTERNAL ANALYSIS

External or environmental analysis focuses on the identification and assessment of the trends that are beyond the control of the company and includes the analysis of the industry to which the company belongs. The business environment is the set of special circumstances accompanying or surrounding the situation or state of the company.

Environmental analysis includes consideration of the main economic, social, cultural, demographic, environmental, political, governmental, legal, technological, and competitive forces that may influence the management of the company.

The business environment has its peculiarities according to its nature and the countries and sector in which the organization evolves, but all companies in the world are affected today by the trends of rapid change, globalization, information revolution, and the prevalence of high technologies.

A striking feature of our time is the rapid change in political, economic, social, and technological environmental conditions. In particular, important political changes that have occurred in the last decades of the twentieth century, highlighting the fall of communism as a viable economic system, have precipitated the collapse of the barriers in the economy and a marked tendency toward the globalization of business. Moreover, the growth of information technology has been truly explosive becoming a revolution that is exerting its influence not only in business, but in almost all areas of our lives. Major technological changes are not limited to information technology, but increasingly new technologies and equipment that radically alter and improve production processes in enterprises are emerging.

These and other relevant trends have to be taken into account by companies in their strategic planning process to determine how they are affected and how they can take advantage of them. In many cases, the strategic planning process should imagine different scenarios or characterizations of the future as a result of trends and likely changes of environment. This process of constructing scenarios involves the simulation of the future environment and forecasts the most likely, worst, and most favorable events.

The analysis of the environment should identify the opportunities and threats it offers to the company:

- Opportunities are the possibilities of a given market (protectionist measures, abundance and low cost of raw materials, untapped market segments, etc.).

- Threats are factors limiting these opportunities (competition, regulations, political uncertainty, legal uncertainty, changes in consumer preferences, and other limiting conditions).

- Techniques usually employed in external analysis include:

- Trend analysis. The application of this technique involves the identification and analysis of major trends in the external environment that influence the future of the company. An obvious limitation of this technique is that it assumes that the observed trends will continue and will characterize the future, although we know that the future tends to be rather uncertain and difficult to predict.

- Simulation or scenario analysis. This technique involves the simulation of the future environment and the prediction of likely favorable and unfavorable events. It forecasts the actions of competitors, the potential impact of these actions on the company doing the analysis, and the company response.

- Analysis of the seven factors. This technique includes a review of (1) Markets and consumers, (2) Competition, (3) Economics, (4) Government and regulations, (5) Social and demographic factors, (6) Technology, (7) Production factors. The result of this evaluation can be presented in an external factor evaluations (EFE) matrix, in which the main opportunities and threats associated with the factors analyzed are assigned a relative weight to highlight their importance to the identity of the company, and can be entered into a competitive profile matrix (CPM) in which the specific strengths and weaknesses of key competitors of the company are identified.

- Analysis of forces in the industry or sector. This technique, proposed by Professor Michael Porter of Harvard University, includes a combined analysis of the following forces: (1) Competitors (rivalry among existing firms), (2) Potential entrants (threat of new entrants), (3) Possible substitutes (threat of substitute products or services), (4) Buyers (bargaining power), (5) Suppliers (bargaining power).

INTERNAL ANALYSIS

Internal analysis or organizational analysis focuses on the identification and assessment of the strengths and weaknesses of a company in all functional areas (management, marketing, finance, operations, research and development, and information) and in the relationships between these areas:

- Strengths are special skills or a company's competitive advantages in a market and internal conditions favorable to change.

- Weaknesses are the disadvantages or weak aspects of the company in relation to competition and market needs and the internal barriers to change.

- Techniques usually employed in the internal analysis include:

- *Diagnosis of the organization.* This technique includes determining internal pressures for change and internal barriers to change.

- *Analysis of key business functions.* This technique generally includes a review of the following functions or features of a company: product lines, sales force, services and retail stores, distribution channels, branch offices, geographic units.

- *Value chain model.* The value chain is made up of a series of primary activities or stages of the addition of value from the general application of production processes (inbound logistics, operations, distribution and outbound logistics, marketing and sales and after-sales service), supplemented by support activities (management, finance, human resources, technology , procurement).

- *7S or McKinsey model.* This technique includes a review of the seven components of the organization: (1) Strategy, (2) Structure, (3) Systems, (4) Staff (People), (5) Skills, (6) Style (management style), (7) Super-Ordinate Goals (Culture).

- *Process improvement.* The application of this technique involves responding to these questions: What do we do? Why we do it? For whom do we do it? Do we know the requirements of our customers? How good are we doing? Are there others that do it better? How can we do better? How well could we do it? How do we succeed? Will our customer be satisfied?

- *Importance-performance matrix.* This technique aims to determine the extent to which the company meets the needs and expectations of customers, taking into account factors that customers value when making a purchase decision and how well the company responds to these values in relation to competition.

- *Competitive positioning.* The application of this technique involves identifying the position in relation to the competition of the product or service offered by the company according to consumer perception.

- *Portfolio analysis.* The application of this technique, which combines aspects of external and internal analysis, developed by General Electric and McKinsey consulting firm, aim to determine the strategic position of the current or future products or services of the company in accordance with the market appeal, the market and the company's strengths, and its ability to compete.

- *Core competencies.* The application of this technique involves identifying the resources and capabilities that provide competitive advantages to the company. This is an approach that is gaining increasing recognition as a technique for internal company analysis.

CORPORATE STRATEGY

Strategy is the ordered set of activities that must be fulfilled in order for the company to achieve its objectives and goals.

Corporate strategy, in general, is the process of deciding:

- The opportunities the company wants to take advantage of.

- The risks that is willing to accept.

- The right balance between diversification, specialization, and integration.

- The use of mergers, acquisitions, and strategic alliances to achieve its goals.

- The sale or closure of unprofitable business lines.

- The most appropriate organizational structure for its purposes.

The formulation of strategies is facilitated by the development of a SWOT matrix type (strengths, weaknesses, opportunities, threats) using the results of external and internal strategic analysis. In this matrix, strengths and weaknesses are usually arranged as columns and opportunities and threats as rows. A matrix of this type allows defining strategies to exploit opportunities and address threats using the strengths and overcoming the weaknesses.

Once the opportunities and threats in the environment and the relative strengths and weaknesses of the company have been determined, a balance of environmental analysis and resources can be made. From this balance comes a definition of strategic objectives (financial, operational, commercial, technological, environmental, and human resources). The strategic objectives should be consistent with the general aspirations of the company, expressed in its mission and vision, and must be established on a firm basis so that they are feasible and compatible and consistent with each other.

Finally, to achieve each major strategic objective, a set of general corporate strategies (growth, diversification, change, development, etc.) should be developed and implemented to leverage the strengths and opportunities and overcome the weaknesses and threats of the company.

ALTERNATIVES TO STRATEGIC PLANNING

The characteristics of uncertainty, change, and difficulty in predicting the current environment require flexibility in planning and recognition of the impossibility of reducing uncertainty through this process. An alternative approach to the orderly process of strategic planning is called the experimental approach, which is characterized by adopting a variety of strategies, keeping those that are successful, and discarding those that are not as the strategy implementation progresses. This approach depends more on sequential decisions than on the formulation of scenarios, as is customary in traditional strategic planning.

The necessary flexibility in the operation of a company, given the changing nature of the environment, has led some authors to prefer to speak of strategic thinking instead of strategic planning, emphasizing the difficulty of sticking to a true strategic plan. In practice, managers must use their judgment to decide on the various real options open to them. Strategic thinking still requires external analysis, internal analysis, and the definition of strategic objectives, but these processes are much more dynamic and occur more rapidly, according to the circumstances.

STRATEGY SELECTION

In developing a strategy, either through orderly planning or a more intuitive and empirical process, companies need to define what their competitive advantages will be. That is how they will outperform their competitors in the fight for their market or particular market segment.

The main strategies, also called generic strategies, that companies can choose from are:

- Low price (some companies choose to offer their products or services at a lower price than its competitors, which forces them to be more efficient and have lower production costs)

- Differentiation (other companies try to differentiate themselves from competitors by creating new products or services or by doing things differently)

- Focus or specialization (others try to specialize in one segment or niche which they consider unexploited or in which they think they may have advantages over their competitors)

Differentiation is perhaps the most effective way to compete successfully, since it is very difficult to remain the lowest cost producer in a market or to exploit a niche market in which no other competitor makes incursions. A company can outperform rivals only if it can establish a difference that it can preserve, so the essence of strategy is to carry out a different way of acting.

The differences between companies result from innovation. Therefore, each day innovation becomes more important as a source of competitive advantage for companies. Innovation is not limited to creating new products or businesses, but also includes trying to create new rules for a market or industry that favor the innovative company.

Besides being more cost-efficient, differentiating, or specializing, which are considered generic strategies, businesses can choose from other competitive strategies:

- Integration Strategies
- Diversification Strategies
- Deterrence Strategies
- Offensive Strategies
- Defensive Strategies
- Cooperative Strategies
- Internationalization Strategies

These types of strategies can be related to a type of SWOT matrix as follows:

- Strategies for exploiting opportunities and strengths (generic, integration, diversification, and internationalization strategies)
- Strategies for overcoming threats leveraging strengths (deterrence and offensive strategies)

- Strategies for exploiting opportunities and overcoming weaknesses (cooperation or alliances)

- Strategies for protecting against threats and weaknesses (defensive strategies)

Let us look at the key features and considerations for each of these types of strategies.

A. Integration Strategies

Integration strategies are aimed at increasing control over distributors, suppliers, and competitors. We distinguish between the following:

- Forward integration (increased control over distributors or retailers)

- Backward integration (increased control over suppliers or acquiring control of inputs)

- Horizontal integration (acquiring ownership or a greater number of shares of a company)

B. Diversification Strategies

Diversification strategies aim to add new products or services. They are losing popularity because companies have learned that it is better to concentrate on what they do well rather than trying to dabble in several businesses. In any case, the preferred strategy is one of related diversification that is focused on businesses, products, or services that have some common characteristics.

Portfolio analysis, as we saw in discussing internal analysis, can be useful in defining the diversification strategy, determining the strategic position of the current or future products or services of the company, according to the market attractiveness and strengths specific to the company or its ability to compete. Other similar analysis or portfolio matrices include:

- The matrix of market growth and participation of the business, proposed by the Boston Consulting Group, in which the products and services of the company are located according to the rate of growth of the market and their participation in this market.

- The life cycle matrix, which shows the competitive position (dominant, strong, favorable, sustainable, or weak) where the company is located in relation to the stage of development of the industry to which it belongs (incipient, growth, evolution, maturity or decline).

- The profitability matrix in which different businesses, products, or services are compared, having the profitability differential and the market share as axes.

Obviously businesses, products, or services of interest to the company are those that have a better strategic position (due to their own strengths, ability to compete, market share, competitive position, and profitability) and are in a growth phase.

C. Deterrence Strategies

Deterrence strategies intend to establish barriers to entry for new competitors. These strategies may include actions such as:

- Very high advertising investments in plants and equipment.

- Financial strengthening.

- Development of new technologies.

D. Offensive Strategies

Offensive strategies aim to eliminate or weaken competition. Examples of offensive strategies include:

- Offering similar products with a lower price and higher quality.

- Aggressive penetration in market segments underserved by established competitors.

- Establishment of plants close to markets.

- Acquisition of control over the competition's raw materials and other supplies or over the competition's distribution channels.

E. Defensive Strategies

Defensive strategies are intended to respond to attacks from competitors. Defensive strategies include the following:

- Position defense (lower prices, investment in advertising, marketing, quality improvement, etc.)

- Innovation (introduction of new products or product variations)

- Attacking opponents in another market

- Carrying out preventive attacks

- Repositioning (changing market segment)

- Counteroffensive

- Cutbacks

- Sale of parts of the company

- Liquidation or market exit

F. Cooperative Strategies

Cooperative strategies are alliances formed in order to combine efforts to compete more effectively. Strategic alliances include partnerships with other companies, joint ventures, mergers, cross-licensing and the use of subcontractors. Through strategic alliances, firms can integrate skills and resources that they did not already have and thus improve their ability to compete both in local markets and internationally.

The following are examples of cooperative strategies:

- Exchange of licenses

- Joint marketing agreements

- Manufacture of products on behalf of another company

- Long-term agreements to obtain supplies

- Formation of consortia

- Joint research agreements

- Franchises

- Joint ventures

- Mergers

For an alliance to make sense and have a chance of success, there needs to be "chemistry" and strategic and operational compatibility between the partners. The key factors are the choice of partner and the commitment of senior management. The development of partnerships is generally difficult and one of the biggest risks is the excess of optimism.

Partnerships must be designed through the following iterative process:

- Defining the strategy

- Quantitative analysis of the alliance

- Preliminary negotiations

- Operational planning

- Structuring

- Management of the alliance

The allies should understand their goals and the objectives of the partnership, agree on how it will be managed, adjust their structures to relate to the new arrangement, and establish methods to resolve disagreements. Lasting partnerships can only be built on collaboration and commitment to the mutual benefit of the partners.

The success of an alliance should be measured not only in financial terms, but in its potential to increase market share, improve organizational innovation, and develop competitive capacity for each of the partners.

G. Internationalization Strategies

Although the international expansion of operations seems a difficult task for some businesses, the benefits and opportunities associated with this expansion are numerous. Not only are there business opportunities, there are opportunities to improve efficiency and quality and a huge potential to discover and implement new technologies and innovations. International expansion reduces costs by increasing volume because economies of scale are realized. The presence in more demanding markets helps a company to improve the quality of their products. Participation in the global market may increase the preference of global clients because of their availability, service, and global recognition. A comprehensive approach strategy increases competitive effectiveness.

Despite its many benefits, expanding the geographical space across borders is very likely to increase coordination, trade, and transport costs and could also generate tariff barriers. On the other hand, a loss of customer focus is likely due to the need to address a very broad and diverse customer base. Additionally, although the globalized business environment offers many opportunities, it is less protected and therefore riskier, which requires a more detailed political, legal, economic, social, and cultural environment analysis of all countries which are being considered for activity development.

In principle, companies should not venture into countries with low growth business potential if they do not have special competitive advantages. If they have such advantages in some countries, they must make the most of these markets to generate and supply funds to venture into countries with high growth business potential, where there may be higher risks. Countries may play different strategic roles as part of an overall global strategy.

Although it is ultimately the competitiveness of a company that will determine their success in international markets, global companies can benefit by defining their strategies and exploiting the competitive advantages of nations in which they operate. The competitiveness of a nation in a given industry or sector of economic activity is enhanced if suitable conditions of business strategy and industry structure prevail and if there is significant internal rivalry or competition. Also contributing to the competitiveness of an industry in a nation are the easy access to raw materials needed and the availability of skilled labor, infrastructure, and technology. It is also advisable to have a significant local demand and demanding consumer expectations. Moreover, the presence of adequate related industries and support for the industry or economic sector concerned is helpful.

International expansion is based on information. Knowing how to learn to act on the global market is what allows a company to succeed in this strategy. Companies need a mental break from schemes used in their local market. Expanding internationally involves developing the capacity in their headquarters to manage international business, investing in the development of management skills in their units overseas, and learning from the best and having the confidence to confront and challenge them.

FUNCTIONAL STRATEGIES

The strategies adopted by a company to achieve its objectives must be translated into functional strategies or specific strategies for each business function that contributes to the success of the overall business strategies. Thus, the company must define functional strategies for:

- Finance
- Marketing
- Operations
- Human resources
- Technology

STRATEGY IMPLEMENTATION

The implementation of a strategy, which is an ongoing task, is the responsibility of the CEO of a company, although it is shared with all other directors and managers.

The implementation of the strategy of the company, besides certain specific actions related to the adopted strategy, involves adjusting the compatibility of the strategy with the other components of the organization. This adjustment results from the need to consider the company as a system of interdependent components that must interact with each other to achieve the goals. Besides the strategy, according to the McKinsey or 7S model, there are the following organizational components:

- Organizational Structure
- People
- Technology
- Core competencies
- Corporate culture
- Management style

All these components must be adjusted, so as to make them compatible with a desired strategy.

STRATEGY ASSESSMENT

Many companies simply measure and assess their performance without assessing the extent to which the adopted strategies are truly effective. It is possible that a good performance is due to fortuitous circumstances rather than correct strategies, or conversely, that poor performance is due to unforeseen adverse circumstances rather than bad strategies. Therefore companies should try to assess to the fullest extent whether the strategies they adopted were correct and, more importantly, whether these strategies will remain appropriate through any foreseeable changes or will need to be modified.

In general, the evaluation of a strategy involves periodically reviewing the environment, the internal situation, and the results of the company in order to determine whether a change in the company strategy is required. To the extent that more changes in the company's environment, internal situation, and results are observed to differ more than expected, the more necessary a review of the company's strategy will be.

A strategy is correct if it:

- Allows the creation or maintenance of a competitive advantage.

- Represents an adaptive response to the external environment and the critical changes that occur within it.

- Presents goals and policies that are consistent with each other.

- Can be accomplished with the available resources.

COMPANY CONTROL

Running a company primarily involves the existence of objectives and goals toward which the action of the company should be guided. In addition, it is necessary to have a control system that allows the actual activities to conform to those that are planned.

The essential elements of any control system include:

- A goal, plan, policy, standard, decision rule, criteria, or predetermined comparison point.

- A means of measuring the actual activity (quantitatively if possible).

- A means of comparing actual activity with criteria.

- Some means of correct real activity to get the desired result.

Modern management thinking puts less emphasis on control, especially in the detailed control that involves excessive intervention in the operations of the organization. It is recommended to decentralize authority and responsibility in organizations, maintaining strict central financial control and focusing the control effort on the results and performance of the organization.

In many companies, control is often concentrated on financial results. Comparing sales targets, operating margins, and earnings with actual results achieved is a monthly or quarterly routine that is done with much effort in most organizations.

In public companies with shares that are bought and sold freely in the market, the share price is often the key indicator or benchmark for evaluating the performance of the company. Other measures such as EVA (economic value added, the difference between the operating profit of the company and the cost of the entire capital of the company in the same year) or MVA (market value added, the difference between the value of the current assets of the business and capital supplied by investors) are also used to determine the profits of shareholders.

In exercising financial control over different organizational units, managers must differentiate whether they are revenue centers, cost centers, profit centers, or investment centers, since the responsibility of each of these types of units should be required in accordance with the finance function they have in the company.

But managers must not only worry about the financial performance and increase of shareholder profits, since there are other areas that need to be evaluated to measure the performance of an organization. The balanced scorecard is one of the available techniques for integrated control of a company, using performance indicators from four perspectives:

- Finance (shareholders)
- Customers
- Internal Processes
- Learning and Change

The development of the balanced scorecard for a business involves the construction of a strategic tree or cause-effect diagram, establishing causal relationships between corresponding strategies to the different perspectives, usually by following this sequence: learning and change, internal processes, clients, finance (shareholders).

CONTROL OF GLOBAL OR MULTINATIONAL COMPANIES

In the management of multinational companies, it is necessary to define the type of control to be exercised by the parent organization over its subsidiaries:

- Open monitoring systems (greater decentralization)
- Closed control systems (greater centralization)

The mechanisms involved in the process of multinational control include:

- The definition of specific and precise goals to be achieved by each subsidiary.
- The development of tools to measure performance.
- Comparing planned results with those obtained.
- Correcting deviations.

The trend in global companies is to maintain only general control of the results in their activities in each country or region, providing local management with objectives, direction, and goals and allowing them freedom of execution. The overall activity requires autonomy in the management of assets and people scattered throughout the countries, supported by instruments of centralized strategic and financial control.

STRATEGIC THINKING

Strategic thinking is the ability of a manager to discern what is most appropriate for a particular organization.

There is no consensus among authors about the exact nature of strategic thinking. For some, strategic thinking is an analytical process, while for others it is a creative process. Moreover, for some it is limited to the process of formulating a corporate strategy, while for others it has to do with solving general problems and making business decisions more convenient.

Apart from that discussion, we can state that strategic thinking includes the following skills:

- Generating new business models
- Anticipating possible situations and preparing for them
- Understanding the relationships between all elements of the company
- Assessing the impact of decisions on the organization
- Identifying trends and complex cause-effect relationships
- Learning from the past

Strategic thinking can be developed by participation in the formulation and evaluation of the strategy of a company, but it consists mostly of a permanent attitude of analyzing problems and opportunities from a global perspective.

By nature, strategic thinking must be systemic; it must be based on a holistic view of the organization. Thinking strategically requires a manager to think like the chief executive of the organization.

Leaders must develop their capacity for integrative thinking, rejecting the simplicity and certainty that is the conventional wisdom of "one or the other", to find new solutions to problems.

CHAPTER 8

PREPARATION OF A BUSINESS PLAN

CONCEPT AND IMPORTANCE OF A BUSINESS PLAN

A business plan is an analytical document for making decisions on how to implement an idea, project, or business initiative. This document must show in detail the development and monitoring of a business opportunity, usually to be presented to institutions, banks, and partners.

A business plan is essential to support a loan application for small business start-up funding, but it is much more than that; it is a guide to help the entrepreneur to define and achieve his goals. The business plan shows where the business will go, how it will get there, and how it will be when it arrives.

A business plan should at least serve to:

- Set goals and objectives.

- Provide a basis for monitoring the performance of the company.

- Communicate the message of the company to stakeholders.

A business plan does not automatically cause any business initiative to become a success, but it helps to avoid some common causes of failure, such as loss of capital or lack of an adequate market.

DEVELOPING A BUSINESS PLAN

Despite the critical importance of a business plan, many entrepreneurs find preparing a written document to be a heavy task. They argue that they do not have enough time to prepare it or that the market changes so rapidly that a business plan is not useful. But just as a contractor will not begin construction without a blueprint, entrepreneurs should not rush to start a business without a business plan. A great opportunity could lead to failure without a business plan.

Before anyone begins writing a business plan, they should consider the following important questions:

- What product or service does your business provide and what needs does it fill?

- Who are the potential customers for your product or service and why will they buy from you?

- How do you reach your potential customers?

- Where will you get the financial resources to start your business?

Following these steps can help in the preparation of a useful business plan:

- Write the basic business concept.

- Gather all the information you can about the feasibility and the specifics of the business concept.

- Focus and refine your concept based on data that have been collected.

- Highlight specific areas of business. Using the approach "what, where, why, and how" can be useful.

- Make the plan convincing, not only to give insight and direction to your business, but to make it a valuable tool for managing business relationships that will be important for the organization.

- Review available sample plans for use as guides.

Unfortunately, many business plans are not well developed and, therefore, do not fulfill their purpose of facilitating a successful entrepreneurship. Most of these plans have too many numbers that are not relevant to making smart decisions and, moreover, are too optimistic. A business plan cannot be a carefully crafted prediction of the future, but instead is a description of the events that may occur and a map for change.

These are some of the key recommendations for developing a business plan:

- Set short-term goals rather than long term (over a year) and modify the plan as your business progresses. Often, long-term planning becomes meaningless because the reality of the business may be different from your initial concept.

- Avoid optimism. To do this, one must be extremely conservative in predicting capital requirements, timelines, sales, and profits. Few business plans correctly anticipate how much money and time will be required.

- Determine the strategies to be applied in the event of business adversities.

- Use simple language to explain problems. Prepare the plan so that it is easy to read and understand.

- Do not completely rely on the uniqueness of your business or even a patented invention. Success comes to those who start businesses with great economic sense and not necessarily great inventions.

MARKET ANALYSIS

Market analysis is the description of the industry or market in which you want to operate. It is recommended that this analysis includes the following elements:

- Description and perspectives of the industry or sector
- Information about the target market (size and distinctive characteristics of the primary target market, expectations of market share)
- Pricing and gross margin targets
- Competitive analysis
- Regulatory restrictions

We comment below each of these elements.

A. Description and perspectives of the industry or sector

The description of the industry or sector in which you wish to operate should include, among other aspects, the following:

- Current size
- Growth rate
- Lifecycle state
- Expected rate of growth
- Major consumer groups

B. Information about the target market

The target market is the group of potential buyers or customers who have common needs or characteristics which the company intends to serve.

The target market should be defined by restricting it to a manageable size. Do not make the mistake of trying to appeal to too many markets. The globalization of markets and companies and the growing importance of electronic markets mean that almost any business can compete with any other business in any country, so the whole marketing effort should be seen within the overall context. As businesses become global, it is necessary to narrow the focus of marketing to a specific segment of the overall market. Globalization is enforcing greater specialization, doing specific things in specific places instead of doing everything in one place.

Target market information should include:

- Distinguishing features. What are the critical needs of your potential customers? Are these needs met? What are the demographic characteristics of the group and where are they located? Are there purchasing seasonal or cyclical trends that may impact your business?

- The size of the primary target market. How many buyers there are? How much do they buy each year? What is the expected market growth for this group?

- Expectations of market share. What is the percentage of market share and number of customers you expect to achieve in a given geographic area?

C.   Prices and gross margin targets

Price is closely related to the objectives of gross margin. Gross margin is the difference between revenues and operating costs. Revenues depend on the number of products or services that can be sold at a certain price. Costs operations are dependent on the resources needed to manufacture and sell these products or provide services.

Price is the monetary value of a product or service. When setting a price, one must consider not only the cost and utility but also all the benefits derived from and/or included in it. The value of the product or service is not in the effort that the company puts into its development, it is in the perceived benefit of the customer.

Price depends mainly on the characteristics of demand, supply, and competition as well as the production costs of the product or service. If there is very little competition, the seller can set the price of the product or service with some freedom, but the quantity demanded of a product or service generally decreases with increasing prices. Furthermore, if the price of the product or service is relatively high, it can stimulate other companies to enter that market. Increasing competition means more products offered in the market, which causes the price to fall to a certain limit, usually determined by the cost of production from a more efficient manufacturer or supplier. Therefore, the manufacturer or supplier who wishes to stay in business should be as efficient as possible in their costs and set a price for their products or services that will at least cover the total costs incurred to satisfy a given demand. The more service or product produced, the higher the market share of the product or service, and the greater the chances of profit.

The relationship between costs, demand, and competition and the constant fluctuations of these factors lead to a continuous variation of the pricing policies of the companies. Price is the most dynamic element of the marketing mix as it can be changed quickly. Therefore, pricing is the most commonly used tool in marketing strategy.

In general, to win you need to offer high quality at a lower price than competitors. However, companies have several possible strategies for pricing their products:

- Price of penetration
- Price of perception
- Selective price
- Price of return of investment (ROI)

Companies can opt for a price of penetration that is as low as possible to achieve the introduction of a product in a highly competitive market and where price is an important factor in consumer purchasing decisions, as usually happens with massive consumer products.

You can also set a price commensurate with the perceived value or price the consumer is willing to pay. This option is generally possible only in special products or services or selective consumption.

Another possible pricing strategy, called selective price strategy, is to initially set the highest price that the market allows and then manipulate the price to attract other price-sensitive segments. This is a common strategy in new markets in which there are no reference prices, or in competitive markets in which it is desired to differentiate the product or service by its price, in this case, above the prices of competing products.

Moreover, you can price in accordance with predetermined revenue and ROI. This strategy can be used in new markets or markets with low sensitivity to price, but it usually cannot stand for long.

Dumping refers to a situation in which a company sells a product or service at a lower cost than the price the company charges for the same product or service in the domestic market. This technique is used to get rid of surplus or to quickly gain market share in a new country or market and is usually considered to be unfair competition.

Pricing policies are decisions which relate pricing decisions to company objectives. In addition to choosing a particular strategy for pricing, companies can decide to provide trade discounts to wholesalers or retailers or grant special discounts to consumers to promote a new product, stimulate the sale of an existing product, or displace competition. In establishing a system of discounts, a company must determine whether they are able to ensure the necessary cooperation of intermediaries and if they are within the law.

D. Competitive Analysis

Competitive analysis seeks to identify competitors by product line or service and market segment. This analysis should include the consideration of:

- Market share.

- Strengths and weaknesses.

- Importance of your target market to your competitors.

- Barriers to entry (regulations, changing technology, high investment costs, lack of skilled personnel, etc.).

- Window of opportunity for market entry.

- Indirect or secondary competitors which may affect the company's success.

A widely used method for competitive analysis is the method of analysis of forces in the industry or sector, proposed by Michael Porter.

E. Regulatory Restrictions

Market analysis should include any regulatory requirement of consumers or the government that may affect your business and that you must fulfill. You must also include the impact of the compliance process in the cost of doing business.

MARKET RESEARCH

Market research is the basis of market analysis and consists of the systematic gathering, recording, and analysis of data on marketing problems.

Market research involves an analysis of consumers, distributors, suppliers, competitors, and the company looking for business opportunities in a given market. The quality and depth of market research will define the possibility of the success of the strategy designed.

Market research aims to answer these five questions: Who are my customers? What do my customers want? What can the competition offer them? What can I offer them? What do they think I am offering them?

Market research is based on a number of techniques including surveys, studies, tests, measurements, focus groups, statistical analysis, projections, etc. To be effective, market research generally requires periodic or sustained application of a set of available techniques over time. This experience will allow researchers to improve their market knowledge as well as their interpretation and prognosis skills.

Market research allows segmentation or division of the market into groups of consumers who have similar needs and preferences. This allows the organization to choose a more suitable segment of the market that has greater value. The subdivision of the market segments requires consideration of several distinguishing features: location, age, income, social class, buying habits, etc.

After establishing the segments that the market is divided into, market research should try to find out what the customers want or expect of each segment or at least of segments of interest to the company. Identifying customers with similar values is essential to designing a plan of action (strategy) that would ensure a sustainable competitive advantage over time. To succeed in a market, it is generally preferable to find or create a niche or segment, usually small and specialized, instead of trying to penetrate the entire market.

In addition to establishing market segmentation and figuring out the behavior of the customers belonging to each segment, market research may have specific goals related to the acceptance of a product, the effectiveness of advertising/promotional campaigns, the effectiveness of sales force, trends in consumer behavior, distribution efficiency, etc.

LEGAL STRATEGIES

When creating a business, one must choose the most convenient legal structure for the business. In general, the following forms of ownership or legal business structures are distinguished:

- *Sole proprietorship.* This is the simplest and most common legal structure chosen to start a business. There is a sole owner and beneficiary of all the profits, but he is also solely responsible for the debts, losses, and liabilities of

his business. The main advantages of this form of ownership are that it is easier and cheaper to create the company, all profits go to the owner, the owner exercises complete control over it , it is easier to prepare your tax return
and pay excise duty, and it is easy to dissolve. The main
disadvantages are that the owner has unlimited liability, it
is difficult to raise capital and find qualified employees,
and the business absorbs all losses.

- *Partnership.* Partnership is an enterprise in which two or
  more people, called partners, share ownership. Each partner contributes in all aspects of business including money,
  property, labor, and skills. There are three types of partnerships: general partnerships (all proceeds, obligations, and
  administrative functions are divided equally among the
  partners), limited partnerships (partners can have limited
  liability and limited participation in administrative decisions), and temporary partnerships (act as general partnerships, but only for a specified period or for a particular project). The main advantages of a partnership are the ease
  with which they are set up, the availability of capital, a
  shared financial commitment, the integration of complementary skills, no special taxes, relative freedom from
  governmental controls, and partnership incentives for employees. The main disadvantages are joint and personal
  liability of the partners, potential conflicts or disagreements
  between the partners, and profit sharing.

- *Corporation.* A limited company or corporation, called a C
  Corporation in the United States, is a separate legal entity
  whose ownership is divided among the shareholders. This
  implies that the corporation itself is legally responsible for
  the actions and debts incurred in the company, not its
  shareholders. The main advantages of a corporation are
  limited liability, the ability to attract financing, corporate
  (not individual) treatment of taxes, and being more attractive to potential employees. The main disadvantages are
  that they require more money and time to operate, in many
  cases corporations are taxed twice (when they declare income when they distribute dividends to its shareholders),

and they require much more paperwork due to increased regulations that exist for them.

- *Limited liability Companies.* A limited liability company (LLC) is a hybrid form of legal structure that combines the limited liability features of a corporation and the operational flexibility of a partnership. Owners of an LLC are usually called "members" and report profits and losses on their personal federal tax returns in the same way they would do in a partnership. The main advantages of a limited liability company are limited liability, lower ledger maintenance costs, and profit sharing. The main disadvantages are limited life (often, when a member leaves, the company is dissolved), and self-employment taxes (the members are considered self-employed and are taxed as such).

- *Cooperative.* A cooperative is a business or organization owned and operated for the benefit of those using its services. Earnings and revenue generated by the cooperative are distributed among the members, also known as user-owners. The main advantages of a cooperative are lower taxes, more funding opportunities, the ability to reduce costs and improve products and services, perpetual existence, and democratic organization. The main disadvantages are the difficulty of acquiring large investors, a risk of non-participation, and the risk of the loss of members.

- *Special Corporation.* A special or S corporation is a corporation that receives special federal tax treatment. The business does not pay taxes, but the shareholders pay individually. The main advantages of a special corporation are tax savings, tax deductions for certain company expenses, and independence from shareholders. The main disadvantages are stricter operational processes and shareholder compensation requirements.

There are other forms of ownership or legal structure, such as the franchise. Franchising is a form of business organization based on a commercial arrangement between a franchisor, who provides the concept of a product, and the franchisee, who sells the franchisor's goods or services in a particular geographic area. The main advantages of franchising are business expansion, brand recognition, consistent concept of operations, training and administrative support, and financial assistance. The main disadvantages are loss of franchisor control, higher costs for franchisees, and restricted freedom of operations for franchisees.

Besides the laws that regulate the type of legal structure to be adopted in developing a business, the organization must identify different legal standards that may impact the business, such as:

- Laws for the industry or sector in which you wish to operate (licenses, permits, etc.).

- Laws for the management of human resources (labor regulations, collective bargaining, unions, recruitment, occupational health and safety).

- Laws on industrial property (trademark, patents).

- Laws on international trade (in the case of a company that will export or import goods and services).

- Laws on advertising and marketing activities.

- Environmental regulations.

ACCOUNTING AND FINANCIAL ANALYSIS

Business plans should include financial information about the company. Financial institutions require both historical and prospective financial information to support the request for funds.

A. Sources of Funds

Companies can gain the resources required for establishment and operations in several different ways, depending on their legal structure. They may resort to external financing for loans or credits, deducting drafts, and may also issue shares and bonds.

Each of the parts into which the capital or assets of a company are divided is called an action. It is an equity security because the holder participates in the profits or losses of the company. When benefits are produced, profits to be distributed among the shareholders are called dividends. If losses occur, the value of each share experiences proportional erosion.

Companies can issue shares of different types:

- Preferred stocks

- Common shares

Preferred stocks are characterized by receiving a fixed dividend collected by their holders, provided that such dividends have been declared.

Common shares are characterized by their dividends not being fixed; they depend on the profits to be distributed and are paid only after covering what may correspond to the preferred shares.

There are usually several ways to refer to the value of a share:

- Par value (corresponding to the nominal value of a share at the time it is issued)

- Book value (will vary according to the operations of the company and is the product of dividing the net assets of the company by the number of shares)

- Market value (the price at which shares are bought and sold on the stock market)

In addition to issuing shares in an effort to raise funds, companies can turn to the sale of bonds or debentures which, while they do no increase the number of shareholders of the company, represent a liability for the company. Usually they are known as fixed income securities, which generate a fixed periodic interest for their holders, giving them the original value upon maturity of the obligation.

The public offering of shares and other securities is governed by the laws of capital markets in each country. The public offer is made to the public sectors or groups resorting to any form of advertising or broadcasting. Usually, laws assign the function of regulating, monitoring, and supervising the capital market to a special body.

The acquisition of funds includes a consideration of the necessary funds and the period for which they are needed. Generally speaking, there are two basic types of funds:

- Passive (fixed rights of third parties)

- Capital (contribution of the owners)

Of course, the acquisition of new resources affects the capital structure. The use of debt in addition to own capital may be desirable if the potential profit of the company is stable. However, external financing involves higher risks and should be used with care.

A decision on the type of funds to be used requires the consideration of several factors, the most important of them being:

- The conditions for the acquisition of funds.

- The financial situation of the company.

- The period in which the funds are predicted to be used.

- The desire of the owners to maintain control of the company.

- Flexibility and the ability to adjust the source and nature of funds in response to the change in funding requirements.

In deciding the appropriate capital structure, a company must consider several factors:

- Analysis of their cash flow's ability to meet fixed obligations arising from securities issued and loans contracted

- Analysis of the ratio of earnings before interest and the relationship between taxes and earnings per share

- Comparison with the capital structure ratios of similar companies

- Discussion with investment analysts, investment bankers, and lenders

The sources of funds to finance the operations of a company are usually chosen according to the forecasts of employment of those resources. In general, regular working capital must come from long-term sources (equity and/or long-term liabilities), while fluctuating working capital requirements typically requires short-term financing. In the case of acquiring liabilities, it is recommended to match the maturity of the bond to the period in which the income producing asset is financed.

B. Debt Management

The debt management of a company may include the replacement of short-term debt with long-term debt or vice versa. Other options are refinancing (requesting a loan from an institution or lender to pay a debt previously contracted with an institution or lender) or restructuring (changing the terms and conditions of a financial transaction). Decisions depend on the existence of such options and the analysis of factors similar to those discussed for the acquisition of funding.

C. Accounting

To make the necessary decisions in the management of money in any type of business, there must be accounting information. Accounting is the way in which a company handles its accounts.

The purpose of accounting is to present the financial condition of a company for interested parties to make their assessments. A company's financial condition is usually expressed in the following financial statements:

- The balance sheet
- The income statement
- The cash flow statement

The balance sheet shows the financial position of a business enterprise with respect to the values of assets (economic resources), liabilities (corresponding creditor rights), and capital (corresponding rights of the owners) on a specific date. Examples of assets include cash in hand or in banks, accounts receivable, inventories, investments, land, buildings, and equipment. Examples of liabilities include accounts payable, mortgages, and outstanding bonds. Examples of capital accounts are preferred stock, common stock, retained income, and accumulated profit or overpayments. The fundamental law or balance equation in which the balance sheet is based is:

Assets = Liabilities + Capital

The income statement or profit and loss statement reveals the changes in assets, liabilities, and capital from the operations of a business in a given period, usually of one year. This statement shows the income and expenditure of the company and the difference, the profit or net income, in the given period.

The cash flow statement is perhaps the most important element of the financial statements of a company. The cash flow statement explains the change in the accounting of cash and cash equivalents. The value of a business depends on its cash flow

D. Taxes

The tax system has a profound influence on accounting and business decisions. Accounting issues, such as the value of assets, depreciation, interest payments, dividend income from shares in other companies, operating losses, capital losses, accounts receivable, etc., must be analyzed in relation to their impact on the amount of tax payable, depending on local regulations. Some expenses can be deferred in a given period or fiscal year to adjust the net taxable income during that period.

E. Financial Analysis

Accounting information allows the financial analysis of the company to be made. The financial analysis includes the analysis of the funding needs of the company, its performance and financial condition, and business risks. By analyzing these factors, the company can determine its financial needs and negotiate with external suppliers of capital.

The financial statement analysis involves assessing the current state of a company by calculating ratios (relationships between two quantities) in five areas of financial performance, then comparing them with the ratios of similar companies. The following are the five areas of financial performance:

- Liquidity (ability of the company to meet its short-term obligations)

- Activity (effectiveness of the use of resources)

- Structure or financial leverage (proportion of funding from creditors)

- Performance (degree of success in achieving desired levels of utility)

- Enterprise value

Although the analysis of financial statements may provide useful information on the operations and the financial condition of a company, ratios have their limitations, so they should be analyzed with caution and good judgment. Comparisons with the value of the ratios of other companies may be affected by differences in size and diversity of the business and the use of different accounting practices and techniques. Moreover, inflation and seasonal effects, among other factors, can distort the analysis. Finally, it is difficult to make generalizations about when the value of a certain ratio is high or low.

PLANNING PRODUCTS AND SERVICES

Business plans should include a description of the goods or services offered by the company and the details concerning the manufacturing, distribution, and marketing.

A. Product concept

Although products (goods) and services are usually differentiated, product truly is a broad concept that includes the services that a company can offer.

A product is the element through which a need is fulfilled. Products are all goods or services that have the capacity to meet the needs and desires of consumers. The higher the level of satisfaction generated by the product, the greater the success. The same product can meet various needs or vice versa. The correct definition of the need to be satisfied enables better marketability.

B. Classification of products

Products can be classified into different types, which must be considered when designing a marketing strategy. One of the most common classifications distinguishes between:

- Generic Products

- Branded Products

Generic products are not distinguished by their origin; they are sold by price and their quality is established by specifications. Branded products have known origins and quality is represented by the product itself.

In general, if a company makes or sells only generic products, without creating a brand, it will have more difficulty retaining customers. The brand promises consistency of quality and a clearly superior benefit, which makes the consumer usually feel some loyalty and the willingness to pay a higher price than the price of a generic product. Therefore, the strength of a brand depends on a strong differentiation and a deep relevance for the user.

Products could also de classified according to their features, for example:

- Durable goods

- Perishable Goods

- Services

Another important classification divides the products into the following two categories:

- Products for industrial consumption

- Products for individual consumption

A product for industrial consumption is used to produce other goods or services, facilitate the operations of a company, or for resale to other customers. A product for individual consumption is purchased to meet the personal needs of an individual. Sometimes the same item is classified as both a product for industrial consumption and individual consumption, according to its intended use.

Products for industrial use can be subdivided into parts and materials, equipment or capital goods, and industrial services. In turn, the products for individual consumption can be divided into consumer products, specialty products, or selective consumption and individual services.

These distinctions between products have great practical importance for marketing because the consumers' behaviors (and therefore the advertising, promotion, and sales management) differ markedly depending on the type of product concerned. Mass consumption is characterized by its dispersion, difficulty in detecting patterns of consumption, purchasing by image (without an objective price-earnings connection), and sales through distributors. Industrial consumption and individual selective consumption are characterized by the existence of professional buyers, the concentration of consumption in relatively few customers, a greater ability to detect patterns of consumption, purchasing by specifications, a high level of appreciation for the price-earnings ratio, and direct sales.

C. Description of goods or services

The description of goods or services in a business plan should include:

- *The design of the product or service* (characteristics, conditions of service, warranty).

- *Production process* (What will the firm produce and what will they subcontract? Where will the production plants be located? What production technology is going to be used?).

- *Planning and control of operations* (estimation or forecast of future demand for the product or service, production planning, inventory control).

- *Quality* (methods to be used to secure and control the quality of the product or service).

D. Life cycle of products

Every product has a life cycle that must be evaluated at all times, because each stage of the cycle requires a different strategy. The phases of the life cycle are introduction, growth, maturity, and decline.

- *Introduction*. In the introductory phase of the product is required to start the promotion of product acceptance. There will likely be losses due to the high initial investment required. For a product to be accepted, an advantage over the other options on the market must be offered to the consumer.

- *Growth*. If the product is accepted in the market, a growth phase will follow. In this phase, rapid sales growth usually occurs and the organization begins to make substantial gains. However, competition intensifies, forcing the organization to incur additional advertising costs, distribution, and price reductions to deal with that situation.

- *Maturity*. In the mature stage, the rate of sales growth peaks, but a decline in profits is also presented. The competition becomes more aggressive and often lowers prices to attract more customers.

- *Decline*. The final stage is characterized by a constant drop in sales, which may lead the company to choose to gradually discontinue the product, modify it, or remove it and replace it with a new product.

Some companies try to shorten their product life cycles and accelerate commercialization, continually introducing new products with short development times. Innovation helps to achieve the objectives of the company, allows greater freedom in pricing policy, and always maintains a line of refurbished products. However, if all companies do the same, the outcome can be inefficient from an economic point of view by not allowing the gains that usually accompany the growth and maturity of products.

Other companies try to make their product a leader in sales in the target market as soon as possible and hold on to that position. They do this because many marketing experts agree that if a product or brand is not number one or number two, it may have to leave the market, unless you have a very well positioned niche. However, other experts believe it is not necessary to achieve the highest market share, citing the cases of many profitable companies with small market shares.

E. Intellectual property

Companies need to protect their products against competitors wishing to copy, distribute, or use their trademarks without authorization. Intellectual property rights protect the interests of trademark creators by giving them property rights over their creations.

Industrial property, in particular, is the exclusive right granted by the state to exploit inventions or innovations for industrial or commercial application. This includes inventions, trademarks, patents, layout designs of integrated circuits, commercial names/designations, industrial designs, and geographical indications of origin. This provides additional protection against unfair competition.

F. Research and development

Research and development (R&D) includes both basic scientific activities and technology development by firms to create or improve their products.

Although small businesses can conduct research and development, and indeed many do, usually only large companies are able to maintain research centers and development units to perform these activities on a significant scale. In any case, every company must analyze the need for such activities, how perform them (independently or in collaboration with other companies, universities, or research centers), and the results they hope to achieve.

R&D can be considered a part of a company's innovative effort, which includes all the efforts aimed at developing new products and services as well as changes in the technical, administrative, and business processes of the company in order to make a positive impact on the market. Innovation has important effects on organizations' performance. Among these effects are the ability to compete, growth and market share, financial performance, and survival.

WEBSITE PLANNING

The internet is an integral part of the new business model. Today, it is almost essential that a company possesses its own website or page that can provide services ranging from simply providing information about their products or services to enabling e-commerce transactions (selling their products and services via internet).

There are now many tools for editing websites, making them easy to create and put in public domain. The following steps are usually distinguished in the creation of a website:

- *Planning* (form the design team, gather information, define the mission and goals of the site, determine the target audience, and establish a work plan)

- *Conception* (establish quality criteria, determine the contents and their structure, determine the graphic format, and create internal working documents)

- *Construction* (design the login or principal page, make navigation decisions, and maintain a corporate visual identity)

- *Promotion* (register the site in search engines and directories, incorporate the site in corporate messages, and exchange graphics advertisements known as "banner ads")

- *Evaluation*

- *Updates and evolution* (maintenance and development)

TECHNOLOGY

Technology is the set of tools and technical methods employed by a firm for their operations. The main technological aspects to be decided upon will relate directly to systems and production technology.

A. Systems

Systems are the set of sequential and pre-established activities that order the processes or functions of an organization. In this sense, the systems of planning, budgeting, recruitment, maintenance, and decision-making are considered, among many others. However, the term is also closely associated with information systems, which ultimately form the basis or support for the functioning of all other systems.

Companies have a number of business information systems that they can acquire and install in isolation to support specific processes, or they can leverage the available technological resources through integrated information systems, planning systems, or enterprise resource planning (ERP). These systems are a set of software modules that enable automation and linking between organizational functions such as finance, purchasing, human resources, production and distribution, etc.

A business' success increasingly depends on the ability of their systems to collect, process, and use internal and external information. Companies are evolving from simple businesses to electronic businesses (e-businesses), characterized by performing all operations via the internet, intranets, or extranets and permanently linking employees, customers, and suppliers. E-business promises to significantly increase business efficiency, improve communications, reduce costs, and bring companies closer to their customers.Despite the extraordinary advantages and the need for modern information technology, the necessary cost of equipment and computer systems is high, as is the cost of software licensing and employee training for new technology. Therefore, new technology poses a significant challenge to managers and their ability to use these resources efficiently.

B. Production Technology

Technology often plays a very important role in the production process. The computer-aided design (CAD), computer-aided manufacturing protocol (CAM) and manufacturing automation protocol (MAP) are some of the major developments that management can leverage in order to provide modern and efficient production processes. However, if an existing company wants to improve their work processes, the use of new technologies requires a precise knowledge of needs, a change in management practices, and the acquisition of technological capabilities (knowledge that can only be accumulated and used by the human resources of the company) for maximum effectiveness. In any case, for the development of technological capabilities, a company must extract knowledge of the supplier at the time of purchase and they must extract knowledge from the production system as it operates.

STRATEGY AND IMPLEMENTATION

Chapter 7 of this book includes detailed information regarding strategy and its implementation that may be helpful when developing a business plan. At this point, just remember two key ideas:

- When creating a business, and directing its activities each day, the most important thing is to know what is to be achieved and how. It is very difficult, if not impossible, for a company to succeed without clearly defined goals and objectives and the identified strategies and resources needed to achieve them. The managers of the company, starting with the chief executive, are responsible for those definitions.

- The execution or implementation of a strategy is also the primary responsibility of the leaders of a company. The difference between success and failure is usually the ability to execute plans. The ability to execute should be embedded in the culture of the organization, its compensation systems, and its behavioral norms. Implementation only works as a collective effort, not on an individual basis.

HUMAN RESOURCE PLANNING

A business plan should include human resources planning. Basic concepts of this activity are found in Chapter 2 of this book, particularly in relation to the selection of people and the legal aspects of human resource management. Let us recall some relevant ideas:

- Human resource planning is the activity of ensuring that the business has the staff needed in a consistent and appropriate manner.

- A company and its dynamics are defined largely by the characteristics of age, sex, nationality, race, religion, social class, and education of its people. Culture, organizational skills, and management style, the key components of an organization, will depend on the decisions that are made to define and choose the people required.

- In every country, there are labor laws governing the management of human resources by enterprises. In the United States, for example, there are such laws and regulations at federal, state, and local levels. These include laws on equal employment opportunities, which protect against discrimination; laws of affirmative action, which require efforts to hire and promote people from protected groups; laws against sexual harassment at work; laws on labor relations, which require the recognition of unions or unions; laws on occupational health and safety; etc.

BUSINESS PLAN REPORT

Although many guides or models for structuring a business plan have been proposed, there is generally a good deal of freedom in structuring one.

Using the main common elements presented in various proposed guides or models, a possible model for structuring a business plan of a company is recommended:

1.   Executive Summary

       a.   The business (What is to be sold? Will the business grow? To what extent will it grow? What is its economic feasibility?)

       b.   People (identify key men and women starting the business and those that provide significant resources or services, such as lawyers, accountants, or suppliers)

       c.   The context (the regulatory environment, interest rates, demographic trends, inflation, and other factors that inevitably change and cannot be controlled by the entrepreneur)

    d.   Threats and opportunities (an analysis of everything that can go right or wrong and a discussion of how the company can respond)

2.   Business Overview

    a.   Legal form of business (type of legal structure)

    b.   Mission and vision of the company (What is our business? What do we want to be?)

    c.   Business Strategy (environmental analysis, analysis of internal resources, strategic objectives, and strategic goals)

    d.   Organizational Design (organizational structure)

    e.   Profile of the shareholders and the management team (skills and experience of the owners and senior managers or directors of the company and those that provide significant resources or services, such as lawyers, accountants, or suppliers)

3.   Marketing

    a.   Market (Who are our customers? What do customers want? Who are our competitors and what do they offer customers? What we can offer?)

    b.   Marketing strategy (product or service, price, location, promotion, and advertising)

    c.   Sales management (sales forecast for the first year, sales force, and distribution channels)

d. Consumer relations (methods to be used to meet consumer needs, understand their decision process when purchasing, and guarantee and maintain their satisfaction as customers)

4. Operations

a. Design of the product or service (characteristics, conditions of service, and warranty)

b. Production process (What will the firm produce and what will they subcontract? Where will the production plants be located? What production technology will be used?)

c. Planning and control of operations (estimate or forecast of future demand for the product or service, production planning, and inventory control)

d. Quality (methods to be used to ensure and control the quality of the product or service)

e. HRM (human resource needs; methods to be used to recruit, select, train, develop, evaluate the performance of employees; employee career planning)

5. Finance

a. Forecast financial statements for the first year of operations (balance sheet, income statement or profit and loss, cash flow, and the breakeven point)

b. Budget (budget or cash flows, capital budgeting, or investment)

c. Acquisition of funds (fund requirements and sources of funds)

d.   Financial management (use of funds, debt management, dividend policy, and investment)

BIBLIOGRAPHY

This bibliography is not intended to list all sources consulted for writing this book. Instead, its purpose is to suggest literature that may be of interest to the reader should they want to know more about any of the topics covered in this work.

1.   Organizational Behavior

Collins, J. and Hansen, M. T. (2011): *Great by Choice,* 1st Edition, Harper Business

Daft, R. L. (2012): *Organization Theory and Design,* 11th Edition, Engage Learning

Hellriegel, D. and Slocum, J.W. (2009): *Organizational Behavior,* 13th Edition, Cengage Learning

Ivancevich, J. M., Konopaske, R. and Matteson, M. T. (2013): *Organizational Behavior,* 10th Edition, McGraw – Hill/Irwin

Robbins, S. P. and Judge, T. A. (2012): *Organizational Behavior,* 15th Edition, Prentice Hall

2.   Human Resource Management

Dessler, G. (2012): *Human Resource Management,* 13th Edition, Prentice Hall

Ivancevich, J. M. (2009): *Human Resource Management,* 11th Edition, McGraw-Hill/ Irwin

Mathis, R. L., Jackson, J. H. and Valentine, S. R. (2013): *Human Resource Management*, 14th Edition, Cengage Learning

Pfeffer, J. (2007): *What Were They Thinking*, 1st Edition, Harvard Business School Press

3. Organizational Change

Cawsey, T., Deszca, G. and Ingols, C. A. (2011): *Organizational Change*, Sage Publications

Cummings, T. G. and Worley, C. G. (2014): *Organizational Development and Change,* 10th Edition, Cengage Learning

Hamel, G. (2012): *What Matters Now*, Jossey-Bass

Kotter, J. P. (2012): *Leading Change*, 1st Edition, Harvard Business Review Press

Senior, B. and Swailes, S. (2010): *Organizational Change*, 4th Edition, Prentice Hall

4. Leadership Development

Bennis, W. and Goldsmith, J. (2010): *Learning to Lead*, 4th Edition, Basic Books

Bolman, Lee Q. and Deal, Terrence E. (2011): *Leading with Soul*, 3d Edition, Jossey-Bass

Daft, R. L. (2010): *The Leadership Experience*, 5th Edition, Cengage Learning

Kouzes, J. M. and Posner, B. Z. (2012): *The Leadership Challenge*, 5th Edition, Jossey-Bass

Lussier, R. N. and Achua, C. F. (2011) *Leadership: Theory , Application and Skill Development* , 5th Edition , Cengage Learning

Pfeffer, J. (2010): *Power*, Harper Business

5.   Managerial communication

American Psychological Association (2013): *Publication Manual*, 6th Edition, American Psychological Association (APA)

Hynes, G. (2010): *Managerial Communication*, McGraw-Hill/Irwin

Munter, M. and Hamilton, L. (2013): *Guide to Managerial Communication*, 10th Edition, Prentice Hall

6.   Project Management

Gido, J. and Clemens, J. P. (2011) *Successful Project Management*, 5th Ed , Cengage Learning

Kertzner, H. R. (2013): *Project Management*, 11th Edition, Wiley

Pinto, J.K. (2013): *Project Management*, 2nd Edition, Prentice Hall

Project Management Institute (2013): *A Guide to the Project Management Body of Knowledge*, 5th Edition, Project Management Institute (PMI)

7. Strategic Planning and Implementation

Bossidy, L. and Charan, R. (2009): *Execution: The Discipline of Getting Things Done*, 1st Edition, Crown Pub.

David, F. R. (2012): *Strategic Management*, 14th Edition, Prentice Hall

Montgomery, C. A. (2012): *The Strategist*, 1st Edition, Harper Business

Rothaermel, F. (2012): *Strategic Management*, 1st Edition, McGraw-Hill/ Irwin

Wheelen, T. and Hunger, J. D. (2011): *Strategic Management and Business Policy*, 13th Edition, Prentice Hall

8. Developing a Business Plan

Barringer, B. R. (2008): *Preparing Effective Business Plans*, 1st Edition, Prentice Hall

Harvard Business School Press (2007) *Creating a Business Plan*, Harvard Business School Publishing

Earth | edition

www.EarthEdition.org